Teaching and learning with multimedia

Multimedia can be motivating and engaging, and it can provide learners with quick and easy access to a wide range of new material. It can also encourage learners to take control of their own learning and sustain their interest. However, multimedia imposes demands on teachers to manage learning in new and innovatory ways.

This book offers an introduction to the issues and practicalities of using multimedia in the classroom – both primary and secondary – and across a range of subject areas.

The book draws on material from a range of case studies and explores areas of concern for teachers and researchers.

The book also looks at broader issues such as implications of home computers and the limits of independent learning, the notion of 'edutainment' and the relationship between motivation, enjoyment and learning.

Janet Collins is at the Open University, **Michael Hammond** and **Jerry Wellington** are both at the University of Sheffield.

Teaching and learning with multimedia

Janet Collins, Michael Hammond and Jerry Wellington

London and New York

38.95

First published 1997
by Routledge
11 New Fetter Lane, London EC4P 4EE

Simultaneously published in the USA and Canada
by Routledge
29 West 35th Street, New York, NY 10001

© 1997 Janet Collins, Michael Hammond and Jerry Wellington

Typeset in Garamond by Florencetype Limited,
Stoodleigh, Devon

Printed and bound in Great Britain by
Biddles Ltd, Guildford and King's Lynn

British Library Cataloguing in Publication Data
A catalogue record for this book is available from the British Library

Library of Congress Cataloguing in Publication Data
A catalogue record for this book has been requested

ISBN 0-415-14897-9

Contents

Figures

Preface

This is a cross-disciplinary book aimed at teachers and researchers in both primary and secondary schools; indeed it is for anyone who is interested in the impact of multimedia in education. Our aim is to stimulate debate so that we can make better use of multimedia in teaching and learning.

A discussion of multimedia is timely. There has been a startling growth in the use of multimedia materials (i.e. ones that combine sound, text, still and moving pictures). The results are visually impressive and the capacity of multimedia to engage young people is not in doubt but what are the implications for teaching and learning?

To explore this question we have worked with teachers and young people in a range of primary and secondary schools. This work was carried out in classrooms, IT (information technology) rooms and libraries, depending on where the school had located its multimedia systems. We carried out several case studies, we presented in-service and pre-service courses and workshops, and we visited many schools. We also looked at what is happening outside of school and became aware of the growth of multimedia in the home and its potential for young people's learning. We were able to carry out several small studies and looked at the ways in which some youngsters were using the discs.

For the most part we have looked at mainstream multimedia products including many which have been reviewed by the National Council for Educational Technology (e.g. NCET 1994a) and others which have been suggested by advisers and teachers or have been reviewed in magazines or journals. We have concentrated on discs which we believe illustrate the potential of multimedia and, although we point to shortcomings in several of the discs, as a general principle we can see little point in talking at length about products which have been poorly produced and which children and teachers do not like. Needless to say reference to any of the discs is not an endorsement; we have not had the space to mention many others which are of equal if not better quality.

In our visits we saw some examples of learners creating their own multimedia products using widely available software. We are sure this creates interesting opportunities for learning and may well have special vocational value or a particular relevance for certain areas of the curriculum. However, multimedia authoring would require a book in itself; as we could not do the subject justice here we have left it on one side.

Multimedia can be used in many different contexts and with many different intentions. It can help create an engaging environment for learners to explore but it can also be used as a toy, a reward, a teaching machine or an entertainment. We are very alive to the particular circumstances of each learner, each teacher and each institution but in our research there were some overarching themes which emerged across different contexts. For example, we found that multimedia can motivate and engage learners and provide quick and easy access to a wide range of material which would not otherwise be available. It can also encourage learners to take control of their own learning and sustain their interest over a period of time. However, this is not a simple matter of leaving the learner alone with the technology – quite simply the much celebrated interactivity of multimedia falls some way short of the guided discussion which lies at the heart of what many of us would like to see going on in the classroom. Rather than doing away with teachers, multimedia imposes demands on teachers to manage learning in sometimes new and innovatory ways. Our work has sensitised us to the problems of doing this – the lack of time, the shortage of machines and discs, the constraints of schools, the demands of the National Curriculum.

We have taken a stance towards multimedia which is, to use a phrase adopted by many of the teachers we spoke to, one of cautious enthusiasm. Yes, we have seen enough to be excited about multimedia but we know that quite a lot needs to be in place to take advantage of it. We have, we believe, passed the stage where we see IT as a panacea for education. Equally, the nightmare scenario – IT coming to dominate our lives and placing young learners in depersonalised and alienated environments – is not one that need come about. Our intention is to stimulate debate on the use of multimedia in education. There is much to agree or disagree with in the book but we hope we are presenting a picture which the reader can recognise.

GUIDE TO THE BOOK

This book is divided into four parts: setting the scene; learning with multimedia; teachers, multimedia and schools; and conclusions. There are three appendices.

Setting the scene

Chapters 1 and 2 set the scene. Chapter 1 looks at what we mean by multimedia and the ways in which multimedia material is stored. Chapter 2 puts the introduction of multimedia software in the context of what is already known about the introduction of IT into schools in the past. This history goes back only to the late 1970s and early 1980s but it raises many interesting parallels and lessons for the introduction of new technologies. In particular it should caution us against making exaggerated claims for multimedia and sensitise us to the enormous barriers and constraints in the way of curricular developments in IT.

Learning with multimedia

The second part of the book examines specific issues of learning with multimedia. Chapter 3 looks at learners and reading and has a particular interest in talking books as this has been one of the most adopted types of software – at least in primary schools. The chapter shows that talking books not only help motivate young readers but also support less able readers and readers for whom English is a second language. However, teacher involvement is needed if young readers are not just left as passive recipients of the text.

Chapter 4 considers another common application of multimedia software – that of information handling. Here we discuss two types of information handlers: the purposeful user and the serendipitous browser. We argue for an approach that gives learners freedom to explore and make their own choices but within a framework provided by the teacher.

Chapter 5 is a much more general chapter which identifies a challenge; how do we examine the mix of words, images and sound within multimedia and, in particular, how do we analyse the contribution of images to learning now that they are a central concern for all teachers? We look at these questions by describing the use of multimedia in making stories, concepts and cultures accessible to learners. We argue that images play to young people's strengths and discuss the importance of promoting visual literacy in schools.

Teachers, multimedia and schools

Part III looks at multimedia and schools. Chapter 6 surveys teacher attitudes to IT and to multimedia in particular. We suggest that many teachers are cautious enthusiasts – genuinely interested in the opportunities that multimedia offers but concerned over issues such as introducing children to the software and finding enough time so they can assess the available materials.

Chapter 7 studies these concerns in the context of the school as an institution. On a practical level this means deciding where to position multimedia systems – in classrooms, in IT rooms or libraries or on mobile trolleys? On a more philosophical level it raises the question 'how can teachers fit materials which have been designed to offer learners choice and the freedom to make decisions into a curriculum which is often highly structured?'

Conclusions

Our final chapter picks up the issues raised in the book as a whole. Software, learners and teachers are three key variables in discussing multimedia and we suggest that the teacher has a key role in using the software to support children's learning and integrating its use into the curriculum. Despite the difficulties associated with the introduction of new technologies into school we are cautiously optimistic that multimedia will be increasingly taken up by teachers.

Appendices

The book contains three appendices. The glossary gives a brief explanation of terms used in the book or in association with multimedia generally. The discography lists all CD-ROM titles mentioned in the book. The list of CD-ROM suppliers and producers should prove useful to anyone trying to get hold of these and other titles.

Acknowledgements

We have a great many people to thank in writing this book. At the Open University, we would like to thank colleagues who worked with Janet on the CD-ROM in primary schools evaluation. Special thanks to Sharon Goodman, Neil Mercer, Peter Scrimshaw, Rupert Wegerif, Shobha Das and Madeline Watson for supportive comments and sharing their insight. And very special thanks to Avis Lexton for preparing and amending the manuscript.

At the University of Sheffield we thank Elaine Millard, Elaine Pawling and Chris Winter for sharing their thoughts and insight into CD-ROMs in, respectively, early literacy, foreign language teaching and geography. We would also like to thank Shafeeq Ulhaq for offering so much more than technical support and Penny Nunn for comments on the structure of the book. Thanks also to Elizabeth Barrett and Nabeel Nasser for sharing their experience of designing and producing a CD-ROM for educational research and to Peter Hannon for useful comments on researching talking books in primary schools.

We would like to acknowledge the help and commitment given by advisers, teachers and pupils for finding the time to participate in the CD-ROM in primary schools project and with our case studies in a range of other schools. Particular thanks to Anna Sewell, Carolyn Freely and Allison Syred-Paul for their ongoing support in and out of the classroom.

Further thanks go to parents who invited us into their homes and reported on the use of multimedia with their children, particularly Jools Duggleby, James Buck, Evelyn Risner and Mark Gamsu.

Finally, we would like to thank the scores of children who have given willingly of their opinions and insights into their own learning with multimedia and special thanks to Ana, Rosie and Hannah.

SCREEN SHOTS

We would like to thank the following publishers for permission to reproduce images from their CD-ROMs:

New Media Press Ltd (Figures 1.1 and 5.3); Academy Television (Figure 1.2);

Cumana Ltd (Figures 1.3 and 1.4); Microsoft (Figures 1.6 and 2.1); SSVC/Broderbund Living Books (Figure 3.1); Random House UK Ltd (Figures 3.2 and 5.1); Education Interactive Ltd (Figures 3.3, 3.4, 4.1 and 4.4); World of Education Ltd (Figures 4.2 and 4.3); HarperCollins (Figures 5.2 and 5.8); Cambridge Science Media (Figures 5.4 and 5.5); Bradford Technology Ltd (Figures 5.6 and 5.7).

Every attempt has been made to obtain permission to reproduce copyright material. If any proper acknowledgement has not been made, we would invite copyright holders to inform us of the oversight.

Part I

Setting the scene

Chapter 1

An introduction to multimedia

We are, we are being repeatedly told, living in the age of information technology. We are surrounded by advertising which describes how this or that computer chip will take you and your family into the endlessly fascinating world of multimedia. This is a world in which you can know what it was like to live on an eighteenth-century warship (*Stowaway*), visit other planets (*Planetary Taxi*) or make choices for Sampangi as you follow his move away from a rural village to Bangalore (*Discovering India*). The message is simple: we now have the technology to inform, entertain and educate. Miss it and you, your family and your school will be left behind.

But is it so simple? Our research has certainly shown enthusism for multimedia products from children, parents and teachers but are we being sufficiently critical of the claims made for many of these products and do we know how we can best exploit them to enhance the curriculum? Of course multimedia is still at an early stage in schools and teachers are just feeling their way to using it in their teaching, but we believe that there is enough reported classroom experience which we can use to start setting out issues and highlighting challenges ahead. However, before we embark on this task we need to begin by defining what we mean by multimedia, to describe some of the technologies and look at the ways in which materials are organised.

WHAT IS MULTIMEDIA?

It is not easy to find a definition of 'multimedia' (see Appendix 1). The term is sometimes used to describe a tape and slide presentation, for example museums and galleries may provide visitors with a multimedia presentation in a specially set aside viewing room. Multimedia is also used in an educational context to describe the mix of video and audio cassettes, printed texts and handbooks which traditionally make up distance learning material. More recently multimedia has been associated with technologies such as CD-ROM, CD-I (compact disc-interactive) and the World Wide Web irrespective of the material they contain. In this book we simply take the term 'multimedia' to be a way of presenting material (often learning material) which involves three or more of the following media within a computer environment:

- speech or other sound
- drawings or diagrams
- animated drawings or diagrams
- still photographs or other images
- video clips
- text, i.e. the printed word.

We can illustrate this mix of media in three examples. The *Chemistry Set* uses a mix of media to provide information on the elements of the periodic table (Figure 1.1). It has a large number of still photos of elements and compounds; sounds made by different reactions, e.g. caesium being dropped into water (see Figure 5.3, p.73); video clips of such reactions; text and tabulated data; drawings and diagrams which can be seen from different angles, e.g. of models of molecules.

Directions 2000 also uses sound, text and pictures, this time to support students learning French (Figure 1.2). For example, in the Lexicon section of the disc there is a list of new vocabulary items. Select from the list

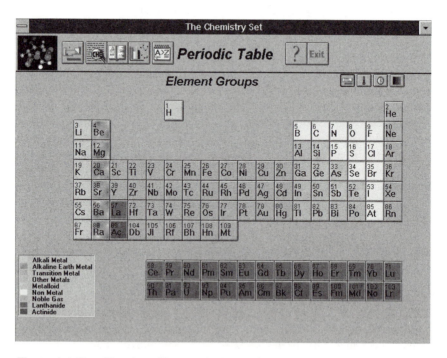

Figure 1.1 The *Chemistry Set* uses a range of media in a disc which can be used as a database, a tutorial program or 'virtual laboratory'

and you can see a picture, for example a one franc coin, a packet of soup, sunflowers, with a sentence in French using the new item in context. Click on a speaker icon and you can hear the sentence spoken by a native speaker. Click on a UK flag and you can get a translation. The screen also has a microphone icon which you can select to record yourself and compare your spoken French with the spoken models on the disc.

Exploring Nature is a disc for younger users which provides easily accessible information about wildlife. It opens with a 'virtual reality' street through which the learner can access reference materials in the library, view video in the cinema, consult an expert to help with identification of a specific species (Figure 1.3) or carry out their own nature study in a park or garden (Figure 1.4).

Smell, taste and touch are also valuable in learning but tend not to be included in 'multimedia' definitions, perhaps because most computer systems have yet to get to grips with them!

ORGANISATION OF MATERIAL: HYPERTEXT AND HYPERMEDIA

These two terms are often associated with the term multimedia, but are not synonymous with it. The ideas behind hypertext were described by one of the early enthusiasts of the 1950s, Theodore Nelson:

Figure 1.2 Sunflowers turning towards the sun (*Directions 2000*)

It seemed so clear to me right from the very beginning that writing should not be sequential . . . the problems we all have in writing sequential prose derive from the fact that we are trying to make it all lie down in one long string . . . if we could only break it up into different chunks that readers could choose.

(quoted by Botto 1992: 13)

Hypertext has since been widely developed and its use in education in such applications as the World Wide Web is now commonplace. The use of hypertext and hypermedia has, since the outset, been accompanied by grand claims (see Ambron and Hooper 1990; Barker and Tucker 1990) which need to be greeted with healthy scepticism (something we have discussed further: Hammond 1995a; Wellington 1995). However, the idea of 'hypertext' has several key aspects which are worth summarising since they form some of the key features of the multimedia currently being used in education:

- non-linear text
- text which can be read or taken in any sequence, i.e. readers can choose which pathway to take
- readers can take 'regular excursions'

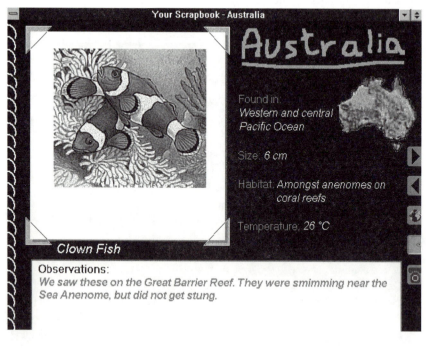

Figure 1.3 Example of work in the scrapbook of *Exploring Nature* (their spellings, not ours!)

- 'hot words' or link words lead the readers on to related information
- items of information are related, e.g. key words are linked
- readers can manipulate text, blurring the distinction between reader and writer.

Figure 1.5 is an example of hypertext taken from the *Schools OnLine* page which can be accessed via the Internet. Here you can click on any of the underlined phrases to call up new pages. Elsewhere you can click on icons in order to download data, e.g. results of experiments, and to post data of your own. You can navigate through the pages by clicking on hot words or by pressing the Back icon on the far left of the icon bar.

Hypermedia offers essentially the same features with the addition of still or moving images and (often) sound. Figure 1.6 shows an entry on Nelson Mandela in the well-known *Encarta* encyclopedia.

The words *Oliver Tambo* and *Walter Sisulu* are hot words taking you to new entries. Click on the loudspeaker icon at the top of the screen and you can see an image of Nelson Mandela. At this point you can click on a play button to hear a short segment of one of his speeches. If you choose the television icon you can see a picture of South African voters waiting to participate in the country's first free elections. Click on the play button and you

Figure 1.4 Another screen from *Exploring Nature* showing a butterfly which has been spotted on a 'field trip'

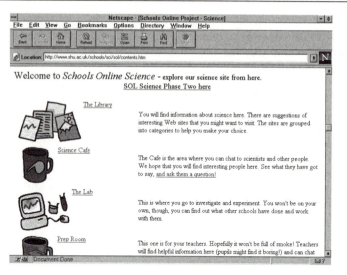

Figure 1.5 Schools OnLine allows learners and teachers to access data, 'post' their own data and navigate their way through a wealth of material

see a video clip of voting taking place, complete with sound-track. The text within the entry can be copied and pasted into a word processor (one is provided as a tool within the disc).

PLATFORMS OR 'DELIVERY SYSTEMS' FOR MULTIMEDIA

Multimedia material may be presented within a tape text slide package or be stored on a floppy disk or may be accessed through the World Wide Web. However, the major 'delivery systems' have been videodisc and compact disc.

Videodiscs first made an appearance in 1973 and came onto the market in 1978 in the USA and Europe in 1982 with the advent of the Philips Laservision system (see Oppenheim 1988). This was a videodisc system capable of storing still video, motion video and audio data, all in analogue form (see Glossary). Its use in education as interactive videodisc (IV) grew slowly and, some would argue, barely made any impact on school education. Several projects funded in the UK were launched to promote and then evaluate its use in education, for example, the IVIS (Interactive Video in Schools) project and the widely publicised *Domesday Project*, both of which are considered briefly in Chapter 2. For various reasons the use of IV in schools did not take off, not least because of the cost of the hardware and of the discs themselves. However, interesting lessons were learnt from the evaluations of IV use that did occur; these can be transferred to current and future uses of multimedia in education (again discussed in Chapter 2).

As a technology, perhaps the main significance of Laservision, or more generally videodisc, is that it provided a basis for the development of the compact disc or CD (Botto 1992). Digital audio led in 1982 to the announcement of CD-ROM and later to CD-I, the latter becoming commercially available in 1992 in Europe.

CD-I (compact disc-interactive) can be described as a 'plug and play' multimedia delivery system, in that it does not need a personal computer (though it does need its own hardware, which looks rather like a video cassette player). Its chief benefit is cost (you can buy a player relatively cheaply) but its major drawback is that it is not integrated into a desktop computer environment – for example, you cannot cut and paste text, or download images or data. Perhaps for this reason CD-I has been seen largely as an entertainment facility for home use. While it has its enthusiasts, its take up in schools has been negligible (DfEE 1996) and it has not been supported by large-scale curriculum projects.

In contrast CD-ROM has been supported by the Department for Education and Employment (DfEE) so that by the end of 1995 NCET alone had placed 5,000 CD-ROM-based systems with discs in primary schools and HMI/OFSTED estimates suggest that 35 per cent of all primaries had them, while there has been at least one CD-ROM-based system in every secondary school for a minimum of two years. Meanwhile the British Educational

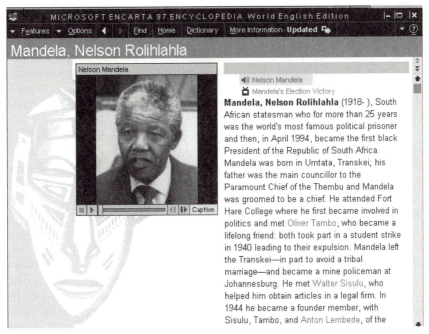

Figure 1.6 Nelson Mandela, speaking for a new South Africa (from *Encarta 97*)

Suppliers Association (BESA) annual survey suggested that in 1995 all UK secondary schools had at least one CD-ROM drive (with an average of almost six drives), while nearly two-thirds of primary schools had a multimedia system (with an average of over two drives per school). The report went on to estimate that the provision of CD-ROM in schools would nearly double within two years (BESA 1995). The BESA report also collected data on the location of CD-ROM drives and satisfaction with titles.

Most of this book will focus on the use of CD-ROM in education simply because this is the system which is currently being used most widely in primary and secondary schools, colleges and universities. The major advantage of CD-ROM is that it can store huge quantities of information in a convenient form for anyone with a suitable computer and disc drive (the vast majority of computers made nowadays come with a disc drive as standard). The capacity of a single disc, and the cost of pressing, will change with technical breakthroughs. At the moment we can think of a single 12 cm disc as being able to store around 660 megabytes of data – roughly equivalent to 250,000 A4 pages of text, 100 million words or 400 floppy disks (each of 1.44 Mb capacity). One typical way of portraying this is to say that the *Grolier Encyclopaedia* of 20 volumes and 10,000 pages, together with a detailed cross-referencing system worth another 20 volumes of space, can be fitted on one CD using less than a quarter of its capacity (see Romiszowski 1988 for example).

This storage capacity is generous but it can still constrain the length of video clips and the use of sound and pictures within a disc. For example, many designers seem limited to around 15–20 minutes of video clips (though much depends on the quality of the required images, the techniques used and the expertise of the programmer). Typically CD-ROM deals with video as short clips, perhaps because of the limited storage space or perhaps because the presentational quality may compare badly with television in extended viewing.

As for the future, there has been much interest in the World Wide Web as a way of accessing material. In 1994 there were perhaps 30 million to 40 million people world-wide who had used the Internet. In 1996 between 1,000 and 2,000 schools had Internet connections; the number has gone on rising. The Web contains largely text-based material but has the potential to include multimedia. For example, the US news service CNN launched a site on the Internet with 1,500 pages of news incorporating sound and video clips, photographs and maps, with the whole thing updated daily by a full-time staff of forty-five (K. Hammond *et al.* 1995: 18). This is multimedia on a grand scale. As a means of access the World Wide Web wins out over CD-ROM because material can be updated, communication links can be built in and data can be directly accessed – no need to send off for discs. However, the big problem is that few individuals or institutions have the technology to download and view the moving images over the Web. The use of the Web raises other issues particularly for commercial publishers – how are they going to charge for materials and when will there be a large enough market to make it worthwhile? In the medium term (say for the next five or more years but it would be foolish to offer any firm predictions) new technology will replace CD-ROM. In the mean time it is, in many cases, the most appropriate means of publishing multimedia material. Looking further ahead, some commentators talk about the development of electronic boxes (computer and television in one) which can be used for accessing on-line services, for viewing moving images including television and on-line video, for communication including video conferencing and one-to-one chat, and as a means for producing and storing one's own text, data and images. Translate such technology to the classroom and the predictions are intriguing (e.g. Keeling and Whiteman 1989). But the task for now is to reflect on the first steps we have taken using multimedia, which we do in this book.

We begin by looking at the use of multimedia drawing from lessons learnt in past attempts to introduce IT into schools.

Chapter 2

IT and multimedia in education
Lessons from the past

The history of IT in schools is a short one – the main events started in 1981 with the Micros in Schools Scheme – but it is one that raises many questions concerning the introduction of new technologies into education. For example, why has the government been keen to support the use of new technology? Have the claims made for educational technology been substantiated? And what have been the barriers and constraints on the use of IT in the past?

To address these questions we begin by briefly considering 'waves and stages' in IT in education and look at the way in which early worries about drill and practice programmes led to a focus on content-free software. We then discuss how, in the 'second wave', people began to classify work involving IT in schools and to provide frameworks for considering the use of computers in learning. We present these frameworks and ask how valuable they might be in conceptualising the use of multimedia. We go on to consider the introduction of interactive video into schools and summarise the lessons which can be learnt from evaluations of IV in education. Finally, we trace the short history of CD-ROM use in schools and the home, and consider the issues which this brief history has already raised.

WAVES, STAGES AND CYCLES IN IT IN EDUCATION

Early days

In many schools the use of computers began with small groups of enthusiasts organising special classes in which children would learn to program in unwieldy computer languages such as COBOL, BASIC or FORTRAN. These programs were first written on punched cards and sent to a mainframe computer perhaps based at a local university or college. Later the whole process was speeded up by sending programs via a modem to the mainframe computer.

Programming dominated these classes but was interspersed with esoteric bits of knowledge about the central processing unit (CPU) or about binary arithmetic, and was coupled with short films and articles showing how computers were going to change the face of education or nursing or banking or any area of human activity you could think of. All this set the pattern for later more widely available computer studies courses in schools (see Wellington 1990 for an account of the rise and fall of computer studies as a subject).

Computers attracted a lot of fuss and interest which in retrospect, but only in retrospect, it becomes hard to understand. Prospective parents were shown round schools' computer facilities, parents raised money to buy more machines, and governments were quick to extol the virtues of computers in schools and to take credit for any initiatives they had funded. Rightly or wrongly it was universally recognised that computers were a good thing. They also seemed to carry a strong vocational message; for example, back in 1981 Kenneth Baker as Minister of Information Technology promoted computers in schools to provide young people with the skills needed for work:

> I want to try and ensure that the kids of today are trained with the skills that gave their fathers and grandfathers jobs. It's like generals fighting the battles of yesteryear. . . . And that is the reason why we've pushed ahead with computers into schools. I want youngsters, boys and girls leaving school at sixteen, to actually be able to operate a computer.
>
> (quoted in Wellington 1989: xv)

But in time it was realised that learning how a computer works, or knowing how to write a computer program, was of little vocational value to the vast majority of school students, who might well become future users of computers but rarely computer programmers. The emphasis on programming was also leading to a disastrous gender imbalance – neither computer studies as a subject nor computing as a leisure interest seemed to appeal to girls. Programming was time consuming and dominated computer use in the class-room and many children could not get onto the machines. In time, the idea of being able to *operate* a computer moved away from the ability to write a program towards being able to load a disk and navigate around one written by someone else. The computer was to be seen as a tool for learning and, despite some very imaginative developments, much of the commercial soft-ware was used to support drill and practice routines.

This led to much criticism of the quality of the first teaching programs and the attitude of teachers to them. Chandler lamented that 'a large percentage of commercial software in Britain is still teacher centred' and that such programs were 'little more than tests and drills' (Chandler 1983: 4). Overall he felt that the situation was so unhealthy that the microcom-puter was making it possible for 'educational practice to take a giant step backwards into the nineteenth century' (Chandler 1983: 1). Similar concerns were expressed by Kelly, who described some 'dangers of misuse' with computers as the absence of any curricular dimension, the use of computers as a kind of educational television to keep children quiet and the use of computers as nothing more than sophisticated teaching machines (Kelly 1984: 4–5).

New models of learning

Chandler's idea of going back in educational practice needs to be seen in a wider context. In nearly every area of the curriculum there was much rethinking as to how learning takes place. The behaviourists, following Skinner, argued that we learn by receiving positive responses to our actions. The art was to shape learning by offering positive reinforcement to appropriate actions. This model reinforces a teacher-centred, didactic style of learning. For example, there would be little point in students working together as this may be reinforcing inappropriate behaviour.

This view was criticised by followers of Piaget and others, who stressed discovery methods. Later the work of Vygotsky, Bruner and others, who stressed the social context in which 'meaning making' took place, became influential (for an authoritative discussion on these changing perspectives on teaching and learning see Wood 1988). These writers introduced a new and powerful metaphor, that of 'scaffolding', to describe the process of learning. Vygotsky's starting point was to consider the learner's zone of proximal development, in broad terms the gap between what the learner knew and what the learner had the potential to know. How to cross the gap? Vygotsky wrote in general terms of the tools needed to help the learning and while these included physical objects (and for today's researchers computer environments) he put a particular stress on language. Through language, learners articulated their understanding and it was the language of those around them which provided the scaffold for learning. Talk between learners and between teacher and learners became recognised as important and writers such as Barnes (1979) and Mercer (1995) were able to demonstrate the critical importance of language.

. . . and yet back to the future?

In the context of these changing perspectives on learning, the idea of simple drill and practice routines in an individualised setting belonged to an earlier behaviourist view of learning and could quite clearly be seen as out of step with modern thinking. This led to a 'second wave' in IT which we describe shortly. However, a recent development, ILS: Integrated Learning Systems (see NCET 1994b), harks back to these early days of thinking about IT, raising the question: does IT change in a kind of 'ebb and flow' motion, rather than stages?

An ILS is a computer-based system which manages the delivery of material to students so that they are presented with individual schemes of work.

Material trialled in UK has included image and text supported by sound, so it fits a minimal definition of multimedia. The system provides feedback to students and detailed records both for students and teachers. ILS thus seems to depend on past modes, or 'first stage', thinking about IT. The program plays a direct instructional role and provides feedback and the pathways through the material. Students work alone at screen – there is little talk between them. In research terms it lends itself to the experimental approach (do those with access to the computer perform better than those without?) rather than the interactionist approach described later.

ILS certainly has its supporters who point to encouraging trial results – but it should be seen as a small-scale initiative having some value at the margins of education, despite being widely flagged and financially supported by a government seemingly intent on confronting some widely held educational beliefs among teachers and researchers.

A second wave

Returning to the late 1980s, a second wave of educational computing – encouraged by National Curriculum statements of attainment – came to focus on the major content free packages, such as databases, word processors and spreadsheets and, at times, smaller subject-based ones such as *Text Writer* in English, *Insight* in science and *Logo* in mathematics (*Logo* was a special case in that it was already popular as a programming language). The argument behind using these programs was that students – usually organised in pairs or small groups – could not sit passively behind them. The programs would work only if the students used them *to do* something. They seemed to put the learner, not the computer, in control.

The rise of multimedia indicates an interest in moving from content-free programs to content-rich or content-heavy (the language is significant!). But does this mean taking a step backwards? Is the material on the disk being used in a simple instructional context or are we extending the learners' control of the software by quick and easy access to the resources they choose to view? To offer a response we need to look more closely at attempts to introduce multimedia into schools and the problems of classifying software.

Categories of software

A number of ways of classifying educational software and its use have been put forward. The earliest and sometimes the most useful classification dates right back to the mid-1970s and was produced by Kemmis *et al.* (1977). Their seminal paper identified four 'paradigms' by which students learn through the use of IT (a paradigm is defined as a 'pattern, example or model' by the Oxford English Dictionary):

- the instructional paradigm
- the revelatory paradigm
- the conjectural paradigm
- the emancipatory paradigm.

We consider each one briefly in turn but further reading is necessary to consider them fully and reflectively. (See, for example, Blease 1986; Rushby 1979; Sewell 1990; Wellington 1985; and see Chandler 1983 for an alternative and interesting classification.)

The instructional paradigm

The overall aim in this paradigm is to teach a learner a given piece of subject matter, or to impart a specific skill. It involves breaking a learning task into a series of sub-tasks each with its own stated prerequisites and objectives. These separate tasks are then structured and sequenced to form a coherent whole. Computer-assisted learning (CAL) of this type has been given names like 'skill and drill', 'drill and practice' and 'instructional dialogue' and has experienced a mini-revival with the advent of ILS.

The revelatory paradigm

The second type of IT use involves guiding a student through a process of learning by discovery. The subject matter and its underlying model or theory are gradually 'revealed' to the learner as he or she uses the program. The revelatory paradigm is exemplified in early educational programs and now in multimedia by simulations of various types, for example: *real* (e.g. an industrial or a scientific process), *historical* (e.g. empathising with a historic event), *theoretical* (e.g. the particle theory of matter), or even *imaginary* (e.g. a city of the future).

The conjectural paradigm

This third category involves increasing control by the student over the computer by allowing students to manipulate and test their own ideas and hypotheses, e.g. by allowing modelling. For example, a model can be formed of some physical phenomenon, e.g. the expansion of a liquid or the motion of a projectile. The patterns predicted by the model could then be compared, say, with the results of an experiment.

The emancipatory paradigm

The final paradigm involves using a computer as a labour-saving device, a tool that relieves mental drudgery. As such, it can be used for calculating, for drawing graphs, for word processing or desktop publishing, or now with multimedia actually performing 'virtual experiments' on screen (see Chapter 5). With this type of software, learners use the computer as a tedium-relieving slave in aiding their learning task. This paradigm raises a crucial issue which relies on the distinction between *authentic* labour and *inauthentic* labour.

Does the use of a computer in saving labour take away an important educational experience for the learner, i.e. authentic labour? An example occurs in the use of computers and electronic calculators to perform complex calculations rapidly. This may be desirable in some learning situations where the performance of a tedious calculation actually impedes or 'clutters up' a learning process, i.e. it is inauthentic labour. But it can also be argued that the ability to perform complex calculations rapidly should be one of the aims of education, not something to be replaced by it. There is a similar debate over the use of word processors in writing – do they ruin handwriting skills? Does the use of multimedia to 'perform experiments' take away the impor- tant educational experience of hands-on science with 'real' equipment?

The distinction between what counts as authentic (i.e. desirable and purposeful) and inauthentic (i.e. unnecessary and irrelevant) labour in the learning process is a central one in considering the use of IT in education and will continue to be in the future for multimedia use in education.

There are other ways of classifying educational software, and types of IT use in education. (These cannot be discussed here but are summarised in Scaife and Wellington 1993: 25–7.) Whatever shortcomings these categories now have, they did encourage a debate around the type of software which should be used to support learning in schools; and as we have seen, the second wave of educational computing came to focus on emancipatory soft- ware and in particular the major content-free packages – databases, word processors and spreadsheets.

It's not what you use it's the way that you use it . . . the interactionist approach

A useful perspective on the problems of classifying software came from Squires and McDougall (1994). In a powerful critique of the checklist approach to assessing educational software they argue that the key question to ask of any software is 'what do learners and teachers do with it?' From this perspective, seemingly unattractive software can promote successful classroom activities. In the same vein, emancipatory software can be used for quite untaxing, mindless activities such as learners entering large sets of data on a spread- sheet. In the context of multimedia, the interactionist perspective would allow us to value exploratory work done, say, with *Logo* on a BBC computer, above button-pushing activities carried out using the latest all singing, all dancing CD-ROM.

By focusing on what learners and teachers do with technology the inter-actionist approach has clear implications for assessing the impact of IT on learning.

For some time we had stopped believing that exposure to computers was to be applauded as a good thing – IT needed to be justified because of its contribution to learning. The theme was taken up by NCET (1994c) which produced a small booklet to catalogue the research evidence that 'IT works'. However, other reports were not always so encouraging. The impact report (Johnson *et al.* 1994) argued that IT did make a contribution to learning but not one that was consistent across subjects or age groups, while a major study on the use of laptop computers in schools was even more disappointing; the impact of personal access to laptop computers on pupils' performance was not significant or at best marginal over one school year (Gardner *et al.* 1992). From the interactionist perspective the question here was not whether computers had an impact on learning but to what use teachers and learners put software and what kind of learning outcomes teachers were trying to achieve (see, for example, Hammond 1994). One particular area of research interest was the role of the teacher. How could one assess the contribution of IT in situations where teachers did not feel confident in using the packages they were being urged to use or when they did not always understand the principles behind their use?

Where does this leave us?

This chapter has traced the brief evolution of IT in education through its different stages, through the attempts to conceptualise IT use and the efforts to measure its 'impact'. There is no doubt that the UK has a good reputation internationally for support, research and development in IT in schools. No other item of educational technology has received, or is ever likely to, the financial support bestowed on the computer since the early 1980s from a range of seemingly competing central sources. The Department of Trade and Industry (DTI) spent £16 million to drop hardware onto school doorsteps from 1981 onwards (see Steele and Wellington 1985). This sum was surpassed by the Department of Education and Science (DES) which invested £23 million in the Microelectronics Education Programme (MEP: notice the 'first wave' style name). The DTI responded with a belated £3.5 million for educational software, and later another £1 million scheme (in 1986) for modems to support the communications facet of IT (these were ten years ahead of their time and largely collected dust in cupboards).

Schools have continued to invest funds (often relying on parental support) in IT, and recently many have been able to buy new powerful 'windows type machines' – the Archimedes, the Mac and the PC (personal computer) with *Windows* software. In secondary schools these have tended to be connected to networks running powerful industry standard software such as *Excel* and

Microsoft Word, giving a further boost to the use of general purpose software in schools.

There has been much to commend in the introduction of IT into schools but there has always been more hype, particularly from central government, than focused and reflective development work. In any case, despite central investment, the number of machines in schools is still small – with the primary sector discriminated against: see the annual figures collected by the DfEE (e.g. 1996) – and even with the best will, teachers have faced an uphill struggle to make IT have a significant impact on the curriculum.

LESSONS FROM MULTIMEDIA IN EDUCATION: FROM INTERACTIVE VIDEO TO THE ARRIVAL OF CD-ROM

What is interactive video?

An interactive videodisc system typically consists of a computer (including a disk drive and keyboard) which is linked to (interfaced with) a videodisc player and a colour monitor. Often the system can be operated by a light pen, a mouse, a concept keyboard, a bar-code reader or a tracer ball, as well as the keyboard. Users of IV can control or 'interact' with the system to choose their own sequence of video, sound, text, computer graphics or even still pictures. IV can provide a combination of images, sounds and computer-generated text and diagrams which, at its inception, was perhaps unique in a learning situation.

Many teachers and pupils saw the potential of multimedia for the first time with the interactive videodisc of the *Domesday Project*. This was a nation-wide project in which individuals, schools and community groups all over the UK were encouraged to send in material about their local community, and publishers and broadcasters were approached to contribute more professional material.

Everything was collated and put on two laser discs. The first contained the schools' and community materials, a mixture of text, photos but not sound or moving image. These could be accessed through navigating around a map of the UK and clicking on the area you wanted to view. Teachers in schools all over the UK took part and for many the most successful aspect of the project involved students investigating their local community. Many schools did not actually see the final disc as few could afford to buy the IV players needed to operate them. The second disc contained full multimedia material and illustrated the potential of random access. However, a draw-back was that the material was presented as a continuous sequence: it was up to users to pick out the topics they wanted to explore by running a light pen over a bar-code. This gave teachers the flexibility to design their own route through the material but was labour intensive and did not encourage the exploratory browsing which hyper-links allow.

This work was followed up by the IVIS (Interactive Video in Schools) programme (October 1985 to March 1987) to develop the use of interactive video in schools. Eight packages were introduced: *Challenges*; *Design*; *Disco*; *Environmental Education*; *Geography*; *Life and Energy*; *Missing the Obvious*; and *Siville*.

Six of the projects focused upon primary and secondary classrooms and two upon teacher education including in-service education (Norris *et al.* 1990). This project seemed beset by difficulties (Megarry 1990) but at least seemed to confirm that pupils enjoy working with moving images. The major limitation of the programme was one of hardware. Schools simply did not have the equipment with which to operate the discs. Rather than be impressed with their design and functionality most teachers tended to dismiss the discs as gimmicks – a justifiable response to their frustration but one which did not always do justice to the planning involved.

Here are four examples of IV material which has been available, has been used and perhaps is still being used in schools and colleges.

Volcanoes   Like the well-known *Domesday Project* this system arose from BBC Enterprises (in conjunction with Oxford University Press). It can be used in the form of a superb database with information on volcanoes and plate tectonics allowing open-ended learning. Here are some suggestions of how the disc might be used with students:

- To look at a model of the Earth's structure. Do they think the model is a good one? What evidence is there to support it?
- To find out how movements inside the Earth can lead to earthquakes and volcanoes.
- To compare world maps of volcanic activity with the pattern of plates in the Earth's crust. One piece of film shows the activity at the plate margins.

Ecodisc   This is the third disc that arose from BBC Enterprises and, like the previous two, runs on the BBC advanced interactive video system. It is used largely in the surrogate mode, by placing the user in a Nature Reserve in Devon (south-west England). The user can explore, investigate, manage the reserve, or simply take a surrogate walk around the lake and woods. Using *Ecodisc* will develop many of the important process skills in science education including predicting, measuring, evaluating and handling data. A full account of the potential of the disc is provided by Bratt and McCormick (1987).

Motion: A Visual Database   This is an IV disc presenting nearly 200 short film sequences of a wide range of examples of motion. It is an excellent resource for a range of abilities, allowing extremely detailed exploration of motion for older or more able pupils or more qualitative study and discussion of motion in earlier years, e.g. why is it best for a car to 'crumple' when it collides with a wall? Why wear seat-belts and crash helmets? (A full review of this resource,

---

which is much more than a straight database, is given in Scaife and Wellington 1993.)

Siville   This allows a surrogate visit to a town in France. For example, users are presented with a street scene through which they can 'navigate' using arrow buttons on the keyboard. As you go down a street, you can enter shops by clicking on doorways and you can listen to a shopkeeper asking if you want to buy something. You need to use the keyboard to respond. The shopkeeper will respond in turn and depending on your choices you will create a short 'conversation'. It provides an impressive and engaging environment with authentic models of language use. However, its limitation is obvious – you cannot hold an authentic conversation with anyone as, first, you have to 'talk' through the keyboard, and second, you can interact only within a fairly narrow set of responses.

This section has sketched the introduction of IV into education. While many of the IV developments were innovative there were parallels with the early introduction of computers. First, the developments were surrounded by a high degree of publicity, often generated by ministerial announcements at high-profile events such as the British Education and Training Technology (BETT) exhibition, which raised expectations and created tensions. Second, they were not backed up with an adequate programme for teacher development. Third, the hardware was scarce in schools and in many cases non-existent.

Lessons to be learnt from IV use in education

What are the important lessons for teaching and learning that have been learnt from studies of IV in action which can be carried forward to interactive media for the future?

One source is a report in the IVIS project which looks tentatively on the educational potential of interactive video (Norris *et al.* 1990). The authors comment on the lack of 'reliable experimental evidence' on which to judge the 'effectiveness' of IT, which in itself is a perennial issue for IT in education and does raise questions about the terms 'experimental' and 'effectiveness'. However, they do state that the 'significant attractions' of IV are that pupils can learn at their own pace, allowing repetition and revision at will; the fact that pupils seem to enjoy using IV; and the reported view of teachers who felt that it motivates pupils.

A smaller but more commonly cited study was carried out by Atkins and Blissett (1990) – perhaps the most significant finding of their observations of six groups of 9- to 13-year-old children is that more than half the time (51 per cent) spent using IV was occupied by 'traditional learning roles' – reading, watching and listening to the system.

Finally, a larger scale study led by Diana Laurillard for the NCET (1994d) investigated the use of IV, particularly the *World of Number* materials which came from another DfEE-supported project, in thirty-five schools. This study produced a wealth of important points for the use of multimedia in education which apply (and will apply for a long time to come) whatever the technology. We cannot do the NCET report justice here, but we attempt to summarise its key findings for teaching and learning.

Three key positive themes emerged concerning the impact of interactive media on learning:

1 *Extended access*: learners were given access to information and ideas beyond the 'normal' range of classroom materials.
2 *Enjoyment and engagement*: pupils enjoyed using interactive media. The increased enjoyment was said to come from the 'audio-visual stimulus' and the 'active nature of their involvement'. They were also engaged by it, and paid attention to it for longer than (say) printed resources, thus making it potentially capable of supporting 'complex conceptual learning'.
3 *Control, autonomy, and responsibility*: the interactive media involved were said to give pupils more 'user-control' and a sense of 'taking responsibility for their own learning'. It allowed them to explore and discover information for themselves.

However, there were some interesting qualifications and reservations. First, apparent activity may be deceptive: 'being active in operating the program did not necessarily mean that they were active in a cognitively productive way' (NCET 1994d: 28). For this reason, many teachers felt that their own supervision and intervention in the learning process was vital. Second, much of the on-computer work was described as non-reflective. The medium seemed to discourage reflection on previous action and results, almost creating the expectation that the user should respond immediately: 'for some children there is almost a compulsion to keep going' (NCET 1994d: 27). Off-line work appeared to encourage analytical thinking and more of a strategic, systematic approach. On the other hand, computer-based work cultivated a more 'trial and error', experimental approach. The report concluded that a combination is needed: 'In order for the medium to be fully effective it is important to combine on-computer activity with off-computer reflective activities.'

THE BRIEF HISTORY OF CD-ROM IN EDUCATION

CD-ROM in schools

Recognising that IV was something of a false start, the government then began supporting the use of CD-ROM in schools. In 1991 £500,000 was earmarked for a CD-ROM in schools, nearly all of which was spent on equipment for schools. Forty-six CD-ROM discs were available to schools, the most popular being largely text based; *ECCTIS* (a database of further and higher education courses), *Grolier Encyclopaedia*, the *Guardian*, *The Times and Sunday Times*, *The Independent*, *NGS Mammals*, *NERIS*, *Hutchinson Encyclopaedia* and *World Atlas*. Teachers in primary schools were not surprisingly biased towards ones with pictorial interest including *Ecodisc* and *NGS Mammals* (see NCET 1992).

The original scheme was followed by a further £4 million in each of the next two years to help secondary schools start work with CD-ROM, followed by £4.5 million in February 1994 for CD-ROM for primary schools. As part of this scheme NCET reviewed over 200 discs and selected core titles for schools. It also commissioned an independent study into the use of CD-ROM in the classroom (NCET 1995, 1996) on which we will draw at various times in the pages ahead. The message of the report appeared to be that, yes, CD-ROMs were welcomed by teachers but that teachers wanted more training in how to use them and how to integrate them into the National Curriculum. The report also highlighted the value of group work and the need for a whole school strategy for their introduction.

A poor relation in the CD-ROM in schools scheme was Initial Teacher Education (ITE). Every initial teacher training institution (ITTI) could receive financial support for the purchase of a CD-ROM drive and applications. In return each participating institution would report back on multimedia use; fifty-six institutions took part. The summary report (NCET 1994e) raised many interesting questions for Initial Teacher Education. In general it drew a familiar picture of a technology which has 'tremendous potential' to enhance teaching and learning but which posed several challenges for teachers. These included technical challenges – developers should pay more attention to designing standardised and user friendly interfaces – and institutional challenges – CD-ROM was quite simply a scarce technology in most schools. On the learning side it argued that schools committed to some kind of flexible learning would be able to make 'best use' of CD-ROM.

These schemes succeeded in introducing many schools and ITTIs to CD-ROM and encouraged the use of core educational software which, while not always to everyone's taste, had at least passed some kind of quality control. An interesting feature of the software for schools was the large number of North American titles, presumably because the market there for CD-ROM was larger and longer established. This marked a move away from the UK tradition of teachers and ex-teachers designing distinctive UK software, often for Acorn machines. Many schools did stay with Acorn and UK educational products for Acorn machines did appear (for example, see one developer's account: Rouse 1994). However, some schools made different choices for their multimedia hardware, e.g. the PC route, which gave them access to a much wider market.

CD-ROM at home

Schools had few resources to invest in multimedia systems or associated software; in some cases this software amounted to little more than what was bundled with the machine (usually the ubiquitous *Encarta*) or with the CD-ROM scheme. However, the number of CD-ROM titles available to the public has mushroomed in size with mainstream publishers getting 'up to speed'. Almost inevitably games discs dominate the home market but educational or 'edutainment' discs are becoming more popular. For example, Dorling Kindersley were able to attribute increased profits in 1996 (of 134 per cent over the previous year) to the marketing of CD-ROM educational titles such as *Eyewitness Encyclopaedia of Nature* and *The Ultimate Human Body* (reported in *The Times*, 20 March 1996). Meanwhile sales of home computers continue to rise. Already over one-third of US homes own a personal computer and over half of these are equipped with a CD-ROM player. In the UK one estimate suggests that 2 million homes had CD-ROM drives by the end of 1995 (various estimates, which seem to vary widely, are given by K. Hammond *et al.* 1995). Meanwhile our own surveys of home use in case-study schools are described in Chapter 6.

Certainly many parents want to assist in their children's education by buying a multimedia home computer and children frequently enjoy the role of being family computer expert. In one sense none of this is new. Parents have bought computers to assist in children's education, often with an unfounded faith in their 'vocational significance', since microcomputers first came out. In many cases the return on the investment has been disappointing – the computer has been dominated by games programs or fun drawing and writing packages. Whatever the merits of these activities (and we believe there are some) the home computer has probably had little impact on children's learning or success at school. This is changing. The home multimedia computer will be used as a curriculum tool. In one small study we talked to girls in Year 7 (11–12 year olds), who on their own initiative made regular use of the *Encarta* encyclopedia to do their homework.

For example, we looked in more detail at a homework assignment on the Vikings. Here the Year 7 girls had been asked to read a short text at home and answer what was effectively a reading comprehension exercise. But the information was missing for one of the questions so the children looked up the entry of 'Vikings' in *Encarta*. This led them to discover lots of incidental information complete with maps, pictures of boats and Viking artefacts (Figure 2.1) and had involved them in accessing data, selecting relevant information and putting it into an appropriate format. It also led to plenty of general background reading. The original homework assignment had called for little more than cued response.

To put this account in perspective: first, multimedia will not create a nation of self-taught children, thirsting for knowledge. Children we spoke to were

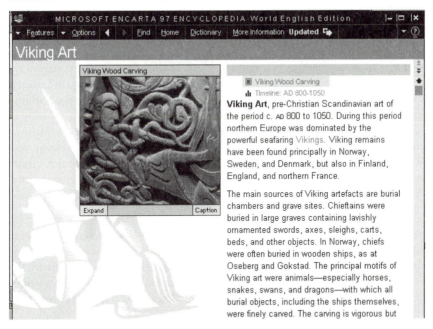

Figure 2.1 Going beyond the task: Viking art (from *Encarta 97*)

not exploring *Encarta* or other programs for fun – these were used as a tool for helping in tasks set by teachers. When it came to using the computer in leisure time, games activities dominated. Will this remain so? So far the market for CD-ROM is still relatively small so that discs are expensive and concentrated into niches – the educational market, tourism, games and techno enthusiasts. The latter market is well served by magazines such as *CD-ROM Today* and *CD-ROM User*. Reviews we saw were dominated by technology and technical issues with readers offered give-away CD-ROMs on Ferrari cars and war planes respectively. However, more general interest CD-ROMs aimed at both boys and girls are appearing. For example, *Rob Roy* offers the viewer a chance to see behind the scenes clips of film in production, a guide to historical events portrayed on the film, interviews and the inevitable quiz. There are dangers here – the history of Scotland can easily become the story as told by Hollywood – but this is a leisure disc that leads you to find out more about historical events and into thinking about the process of film production.

Second, access to multimedia poses issues of equity which cannot be ignored. Quite simply, not everyone can afford a home computer. This threatens to add to the gap in educational achievement between 'haves' and 'have nots'. One way of addressing the issue is to make sure that school and homework do not require multimedia materials. But we have already found that children will use multimedia on their own initiative and in many cases unknown to their teachers. In any case ignoring multimedia threatens to lead to a fossilised curriculum. The problem can be addressed only by large-scale provision of multimedia in schools and public libraries – although, in honesty, we should recognise that is unlikely to happen on anything like the required scale.

Once again, as with so many issues in IT in education, the problem of equity is a perennial and recurrent one. In the mid-1980s Hannon and Wooler (1985) warned that the 'gulf between children of different classes will widen'. Even if equal access to IT at school or college could be ensured (and there are still no grounds for optimism on this), huge differences would continue in home access and use. The authors predicted that:

> Entire curricula are likely to be marketed by software houses or large publishing corporations. The result will be fatal to the opportunities of many working class children who will be disadvantaged in terms of the sheer amount of time they will be able to spend learning via computers. Economic differences between families are likely to be translated even more directly into educational differences.
>
> (Hannon and Wooler 1985: 93)

This has already happened with the major push by Dorling Kindersley and other publishing houses into the home multimedia market, with titles covering large parts of the National Curriculum, most notably history, geography, science and technology.

SUMMARY AND DISCUSSION

Access to computers is still quite closely rationed in most schools but there has been a huge growth in the physical presence of IT starting from a very low base in the early 1980s. We have seen a rise in the number of industry standard, Windows-type machines and a growth of powerful, general purpose programs, often content-free and 'exploratory' software (ILS notwithstanding). Now we are seeing the introduction of multimedia CD-ROMs. IT has come a long way but what lessons can we learn from the journey taken so far?

The first point to emerge is that the use of IT has been characterised by false starts (e.g. computer studies) and changes of direction (e.g. the development and decline of IV, moves to and away from content-free software). There is nothing wrong with change in itself but there is clearly a need for more critical thinking about the value and use of IT in schools. The alternative is to be left at the mercy of each passing fad and fancy. But how best to achieve this critical perspective? The simple solution is to set up controlled experiments and see if learners using IT outscore learners without IT. But this will not work. It is always difficult to compare two sets of learners – so much depends on the settings in which learning is taking place. Research into IT poses further methodological problems as children learn different things using IT so that learning outcomes cannot be easily compared. In any case we have seen that it is what you do with IT that counts, not IT in itself that makes a difference. Context is everything and this leads us to look at the key classroom variables of learner, teacher and software. What do we know about each of these and what critical questions remain regarding the use of multimedia?

Learners and IT

We know that learners in general enjoy using computers and that they are motivated and engaged by multimedia material. Research further suggests that multimedia (along with other IT) can widen learners' experiences by giving them access to activities which would be impossible or time consuming to organise in other ways. Finally, IT can provide opportunities for learners to take more control over their learning and accept more responsibility.

However, some of this needs further exploration. How do learners engage with multimedia? How do learners engage with text in a multimedia environment and what do they learn from images? Does motivation arise from pushing buttons and seeing things happen or is there something deeper going on?

We also need to know more about accessing multimedia material – do learners hop at random from screen to screen or are they doing something more purposeful?

Software

We have seen that there has been some value in using categories to describe different types of software as it draws attention to what the software was designed to do. We know that some categories of software have been recommended more strongly for use in the classroom. In particular, there have been repeated worries (at least from educationalists) about the use of instructional software and we know that new project materials have often favoured a more learner-centred approach. For example IVIS project materials made heavy use of databases (emancipatory software) and simulations. But do we have ways of categorising multimedia software and what will new software look like?

Teachers

We know that hardware and software have in the past been dumped on teachers without proper explanation or time given for reflection on how they can best be used. In addition we know that teachers are faced with a challenge in getting to grips with the technical features of IT. We also know that teachers often find it difficult to support more learner-centred teaching styles even if these may be precisely the styles favoured by many software designers. This may lead teachers to impose a structure on the use of software (through worksheets) even if they might not actually stand over students to supervise its use. New software is often resisted or assimilated and as Latchem *et al.* (1993: 28) note, 'despite all the advances and investment in the technology, computers have not radically changed classroom pedagogies and are typically used to add to existing practice rather than replace it'. Critical questions raised now are how do teachers learn to use multimedia and how do they incorporate multimedia into their teaching?

Finally, we know something about the difficulties learners have in taking responsibility for their learning; one report concludes 'few students are able to optimise their own learning' (Atkins 1993: 260). What role then does the teacher have in supporting learners using multimedia?

And the future . . .

Teachers often have to fit their use of IT within the physical and cultural constraints of institutions. In part this means organising access to scarce machines which may not be located in the most convenient places for teachers wanting to make use of them. But there is more. At least in the UK there is increasing pressure on schools to teach to an externally validated National Curriculum with traditional forms of assessment. When computer meets school there are no prizes for guessing who wins. Yet here we have a contradiction. Despite the constraints and difficulties of introducing IT into schools, and all the pressures that teachers are under, the momentum has not died away. Parents, government, political parties and many teachers are as committed to IT as ever. We have to understand this commitment in the context of our rapidly changing world. IT is commonplace in work and in homes, growing numbers of people have access to multimedia and are linking up to the Internet. What impact will these changes have on the future curriculum?

The questions we have raised in this summary underpin the discussions in the following chapters. Chapters 3, 4 and 5 focus in particular on learners and software, Chapters 6 and 7 consider teachers and institutions. The final chapter provides an overview of the book and explicitly addresses the critical questions we have raised here. First, then, we look at learners and multimedia and start with children learning to read.

Part II

Learning with multimedia

Chapter 3

Learners and reading

In this chapter we look at talking books (i.e. stories that are backed up with animation and sound-track) as this is an area which has caught the interests of many primary school teachers and their pupils. We raise some general issues of the role of the teacher, or parent, in supporting children using multimedia texts and the ways in which learners interact with the text. After a brief account of what it is to be a reader we describe the talking books which were the focus of small-scale case studies. These studies of children working in school and at home illustrate the way in which talking books can be used to support the mechanics of reading and help to motivate children to want to read. We conclude the chapter with a discussion of the limitations of currently available software and highlight areas for development.

READING

It is a widely held belief that children need to read to take their place in society. Being a reader involves so-called functional literacy which is the ability to read messages and decode instructions, labels and signs. However, it also involves being able to read and have access to knowledge contained in articles and textbooks and engaging with literature for pleasure, self-discovery and self-realisation 'which most English teachers accept as an integral and central component in any conception of education' (Millard 1994: 37). In our view, teachers should aim 'to help children become readers who see books as an important part of their lives and who will continue to enjoy literature as they grow up' (Bennett 1979: 3). This involves more than reading at a functional level. In addition to a mastery of the mechanics of reading, being a reader is also concerned with having a reading habit, of deriving pleasure from what is read while at the same time developing and applying a critical awareness, a willingness to probe further, to have an understanding which goes beyond the words on the page.

In this chapter we consider the ways in which talking books can support the teaching of reading, or more precisely the way in which talking books can enable children to learn to read and become readers. This is not merely a question of semantics.

> Children can not be taught to read. A teacher's responsibility is not to teach children to read but to make it possible for them to learn to read.
>
> (Smith 1978: 6)

This process involves providing children with appropriate decoding skills using phonic, whole word and context clues while, at the same time, encouraging them to enjoy stimulating texts which allow them to behave like readers. Consequently, we are interested in how talking books teach children the mechanics of the reading process while at the same time motivating children to want to read. Talking books seem to offer tremendous potential in the teaching of reading. First, because they can be used in much the same way as traditional print-based text programmes they can support a wide range of current approaches to reading. This means there is no difficulty in integrating them into existing reading programmes:

> The real attraction of electronic books is that they can fit into the way teachers teach reading, rather than forcing teachers to change to accommodate the technology.
>
> (Medwell 1995: 24)

Second, they are easy and fun to use which motivates children to want to use them. Finally, multimedia texts can be used to great effect to support both beginners and less able readers.

TALKING BOOKS

In this chapter we focus on some of the CD-ROM titles which were recommended in the NCET (1994a) reviews and are therefore widely used in schools. These include *The Paper Bag Princess, Heather Hits a Home Run, Moving Gives Me a Stomach Ache* (from the series *Kids Can Read*), *Just Grandma and Me, The Tortoise and the Hare* (from the series *Living Books*) and *Sherston's Naughty Stories*. The first five titles were made in the USA and are read with recognisable North American accents. All these titles have long been available and popular as paper-based books.

With the *Kids Can Read* series children can see the text and pictures of the original story and they can click on a loudspeaker icon to hear the texts spoken in English or Spanish. (These North American titles include the Spanish option for the large hispanic-American community.) By clicking on an individual word in the text the children can hear it spoken. This facility can be 'customised' so as to give an explanation of the meaning of the word, a grammatical description of the word and also its Spanish equivalent. Children can click on pictures in the story and a word materialises. For example click on a brick and the word brick appears; again this can be customised so that the word is spoken and sometimes a sound effect is produced. The size and font of the text can also be customised.

With both *Living Books* and *Sherston's Naughty Stories* children can also view the text and pictures of the original story. Children can click on the appropriate icon to hear the whole text or they can click on individual words to hear how they are pronounced. Opportunities to customise these discs are limited or non-existent. However, one of the key features of *Living Books* and *Sherston's Naughty Stories* is the presence of 'hot spots' which, when clicked, produce animation. For example, on one page of *Just Grandma and Me,* Grandma and the (asexual) child are on the beach (Figure 3.1). Click on a shell and a crab comes out and snaps at the child, click on the other characters on the beach and one plays in the sand, another picks up the sun oil and a third hops up and down on the hot sand. Click on another shell and it starts dancing, click on the beach cabin and a voice from inside says 'just a minute', click on Grandma and she turns over the page of her book, click on the child and 's/he' taps at a shell.

Using these discs with primary school children convinced us that some multimedia texts were highly motivating and thus had an important role to play in allowing them to become readers. However, we became increasingly aware that no material, not even the best software, can be used effectively

Figure 3.1 *Just Grandma and Me* allows children to listen to the story as they read

without clear guidance from a teacher (or parent). In our experience children did not spontaneously talk to each other about the stories as they were reading them. It was only when they retold the story in front of an interested adult that the children spoke fluently about the stories and would spontaneously mime and act out parts of the stories. Similarly, without direct intervention from a teacher, children were unlikely to support their reading of the text by clicking on individual words that they did not know. This suggests that teachers and other adults have an important role to play in supporting children's use of talking books. As with traditional print-based materials, talking about the story is as important for young children as reading the words on the page.

Our approach to the teaching of reading is based on the assumption that learning to read involves similar processes as learning to speak. Adults enable children to learn to speak by talking to them.

> Gradually he begins to talk back, and because you want him to join in a dialogue with you and the rest of the family you don't mind if you do most of the talking and he answers with only one or two words. ... You help him, letting him take over a bigger share of the conversation. You encourage him by responding and he learns to talk by talking.
>
> (Meek 1982: 21)

The adult's role is to read with the child, to help them observe what there is to be read, and to tell them what they need to know when they find it difficult. In our opinion, this kind of adult support is as important with talking books as it is with other applications of multimedia in education and with more traditional print-based materials.

SUPPORTING THE MECHANICS OF READING

Talking books are accessible and highly motivating but do they help children to develop specific reading skills? We believe that they have the potential to develop reading skills by giving children an overview of a story prior to reading it, by supporting children's independent reading through sounding out unrecognised words and by encouraging collaborative reading in front of a public 'page'. However, our work with children in primary schools suggests that this potential is rarely realised. Effective use of the software is dependent on the teacher providing appropriate support or 'scaffolding' learning.

The need for appropriate teacher intervention is highlighted in the following account of using talking books to teach reading to less able and bilingual learners.

First case-study school

The school is close to the centre of a city in northern England, and caters for over 200 pupils aged between 4 and 10. The school has a significant proportion of bilingual pupils and pupils who are just beginning to learn English. It also has a unit catering for children with emotional and behavioural difficulties, and the majority of the children in the school are considered by the staff to have special educational needs. The school's CD-ROM system is moved from classroom to classroom and during our visit was located in an open area between two infant classrooms. Because this is a rather noisy area, speakers had been fitted to the machine.

The 5, 6 and 7 year olds we observed were timetabled to have access to the CD-ROM for four weeks. The teacher began with a whole class demonstration of *Sherston's Naughty Stories*. On this occasion the teacher encouraged the children to read each page of text for themselves before hearing the story read to them. The children were also encouraged to activate the screen's hot spots before turning the page. Although this demonstration provided the children with a clear structure for 'reading' the text, the emphasis on the mechanics of operating the software did little to encourage exploratory talk about the story. After the demonstration, pairs or groups of children (selected from a flexible rota) were given time to read some stories for themselves. It was intended that this activity would familiarise pupils with the CD-ROM and develop IT skills, while also providing structured reading activity. Indeed, as a structured exercise the activity worked extremely well with many of the children being able to read the stories. However, there was little discussion about the stories either while the children were working on the computer or immediately afterwards. Listening to the pupils' accurate, but slightly stilted, reading of the *Naughty Stories* emphasised the importance of providing opportunities for children to talk about the texts they read.

The first group were initially made up of four girls. Nancy and Lana (both aged 5) were close friends who often worked together. Tamasina and Anna (aged 7) were both Farsi speakers. Both had only recently come to the UK. Anna spoke very little English and depended on Tamasina (whose English was much better) to translate for her. These girls were later joined by a 5-year-old boy, Hussein (also a Farsi speaker, with limited English). There was some discussion as they listened to/read/watched the story, though the three fluent English speakers tended to dominate the discussion. The three English speakers read the story aloud before they used the mouse to activate the recorded voice. The children spent a couple of minutes listening to the story and exploring each page before moving on to the next. Clicking on the pictures did not sustain their interest and the time spent on each page declined as the story progressed. Lana was the only one who commented on events in the story. Tamasina often translated the text for Anna and Hussein. The children often supported each other's reading with comments like 'well done'. They took it in turns to control the mouse, without dispute.

The fact that some children could read the stories meant that there was no need for them to click on individual words. Indeed, the pupils seemed reluctant to use the technology to support their reading. When they got stuck, their first response was to help each other. They seemed reluctant to access help from the technology and they clicked the word on the screen only as a last resort. They were in Jane Medwell's (1994) term 'reluctant clickers'. This meant that surprisingly few words were clicked and with some stories the children went through the entire story without clicking on any words at all.

The facility of clicking on individual words seems to be far more appropriate when children tackle texts which they find difficult. For example, being able to hear individual words enabled a group of more able pupils to persevere for thirty minutes with *The Paper Bag Princess* which was, for them, a difficult text. In a further attempt to support the children's reading the *Kids Can Read* series was used to give simple definitions of words along with their pronunciations. However, in most cases these definitions did not help as they were not pitched at the right level. For example, in the story *Heather Hits a Home Run* a 'tee' was described as 'a small peg on which a ball is placed and off which it is struck' but, not surprisingly, the children could not understand what this meant. Fortunately some pairs decided to click on the tee in the picture and were thus able to link the word with the object. The fact that the children persevered with, and seemed to enjoy, these books despite the difficulties that they experienced in reading and understanding the text highlights the role of the teacher both in choosing appropriate texts and providing necessary support.

When using *Sherston's Naughty Stories* the teacher was frequently busy with the rest of the class, often in other parts of the school, and could make very little input. Children sometimes experienced difficulty in accessing their chosen story, probably because the process of selection was not explained within the software. The children succeeded largely by trial and error, and by ignoring the seemingly random messages which appeared in 'dialogue boxes' on the screen. Not surprisingly the teacher could offer no explanation for the appearance of these messages. Both pupils and teacher accepted them as an inevitable aspect of the software with the teacher commenting, 'Well, computers are like that, aren't they?'

This school is having some success in making CD-ROM activities accessible to children with limited command of written English, and doing so in ways that might be expected to help their English literacy development. It seemed clear, however, that teachers had not had much time to explore the educational potential of the *Naughty Stories* software, and needed to rely on the ability and willingness of pupils to take an active role in using it. As Carol Burns (1995) points out, talking books are designed to be used by young children without teacher assistance.

However, whenever children use a computer with adult help, the language experience will be enriched, and so on the occasions when an adult was available, the interchange of language was much enhanced by different aspects of questioning and checking the children's understanding.

(Burns 1995: 18)

Her account of the discussion generated about the characters and their antics in *Naughty Stories* is in sharp contrast to the slightly stilted readings we observed when children were working without adult intervention.

MOTIVATING READERS

Even the briefest of observations can leave one in no doubt that multimedia texts can be extremely motivating for children of all ages. Collins and her colleagues (NCET 1996) reported on examples in which children as young as 5 were observed working with talking books for over half an hour at a time. Based on her work in a reception class Carol Burns (1995: 16) comments how 'the excitement and novelty of it kept everyone sitting patiently, for a change'. High levels of motivation are created and sustained as children listen to the story and find hot spots which activate a number of animations on each page. As well as being enjoyable, talking books are extremely accessible with most children being able to navigate their way through the predominantly intuitive structures.

The motivational effect of these animations became obvious when in the second case-study school we watched pupils reading *Just Grandma and Me* and *The Tortoise and the Hare*.

Second case-study school

Our observations took place in a northern school which is extremely popular with local parents. The school attracts a number of 'professional families' without being uniformly white or middle class. Most of the children in the class of 6 year olds are confident readers and have a wide selection of both reading scheme and 'real' books from which to choose. All the children knew how a story worked and had sufficient phonic awareness to be able to decode words in context. The class had access to a multimedia machine to use for half a term. The children were shown how to load the discs and navigate through the material before working in pairs reading the stories for themselves. The teacher did not intervene while the children worked on the computer, but she did talk to the children about what they had read and direct them to follow-up activities. Thus the children's reading of the talking books provided a stimulating introduction to their own verbal, written and illustrated versions of the stories. The teacher described the books that the children produced as a result of using the CD-ROM as some of the best writing which the children had done in terms of imagination, length of text and sequencing.

When reading the stories each pair of children followed the story in similar ways. Having listened to the automatic reading of the text the children then tried to find the hot spots. They frequently made suggestions to each other such as 'Why don't you do the fence?' or 'Go on, click the tortoise'. However, they did not discuss the story line with each other and rarely commented on the actions of the characters on screen other than to laugh and say 'That's funny'.

While the animations did not necessarily generate discussion of the story line our subsequent conversations with the children suggest that they enhanced the children's experience of reading the story.

> Where there is real integration of the images and the message the two form an invisible whole: there is a harmony which strengthens the impact on the reader. Meaning is absorbed from the whole experience and unknown language and unfamiliar syntax do not become insurmountable obstacles to understanding.
>
> (Fremantle 1993: 15)

Sometimes the animations had a direct functional value. For example on 'page' 6 of *The Tortoise and the Hare* the verbs 'hop, skip, jump, sprint and lope' are illustrated amusingly through the antics of the hare. Moreover, as Mary explained, the animations also help to reinforce the point of the story.

> If you don't click on things it doesn't seem like the hare and the tortoise are racing . . . it's like they're walking across the field not having a race.

Rather than being merely gimmicks, some hot spots actually encouraged the children to read beyond the text on the page (Figure 3.2). For example, in one scene from *The Tortoise and the Hare* the tortoise is lying in a wood where birds sing, a frog plays double bass, a lizard plays guitar and the beaver pounds out a rhythm on the drum. The hare meets the tortoise and says, 'What a lazy life you must have, at this rate how can you get anything done?' However, while the hare believes that the tortoise is wantonly idle, the on-screen animation offers an alternative view that the tortoise is, in fact, at peace in an environment which is meant to be enjoyed. The animations ensure that we feel some sympathy with the tortoise. As one child said, 'I would like to be there, I would have a picnic and jump on the rock'.

Unfortunately not all screen animations are as thought provoking as the examples cited above. While some of the animations in *Just Grandma and Me* enhance the story line, others do not. The better animations of the beach scenes could lead children to invent a series of parallel stories for the different characters that appear there. They certainly add a great deal to an appreciation of what one might see during a day at the beach. However, other animations, such as the fence that dances while Grandma and the child wait

Figure 3.2 As demonstrated in *The Tortoise and the Hare,* animations can reinforce the point of the story

for the bus, add nothing at all to the story. Plowman (1996) criticises activities that bear only a tangential relationship to the narrative as a source of 'fragmentation' which detracts from children's understanding of the story.

> Copious opportunities for machine interaction do not necessarily make for quality interaction: some of these can be examples of gratuitous interactivity, others can be detrimental to group dynamics of the unfolding narrative.
>
> (Plowman 1996: 98)

Possible distractions such as these add to the concerns of people like the educational journalist who asks 'how likely is it that a child left alone will play with the words rather than the pictures?' (Coren 1994).

Accessibility of talking books

Irrespective of their relevance to the story line, animations certainly make talking books popular with children. The accessibility of talking books and the fact that they can be used by even young children adds to their attraction. Indeed, talking books are so popular with children that, in many schools, time on the computer is being used as a reward for good behaviour both at playtimes and during lessons.

> When we have been good we have a 'special day' when we can choose
> what we want to do. Me and my friends always choose to play on the
> CD-ROM reading stories and things.
>
> (Primary school pupil)

The attraction of interactive multimedia texts means that the software is
being used by a wide age range of children with very differing abilities. As
with the earlier emphasis on picture books for older readers, the introduction of talking books has provided less able readers with access to simpler
texts without the stigma of being seen to read 'baby books'. This can be
particularly important for pupils with special educational needs in mainstream classrooms.

> I would say that every class from 5 to 11 has used *Naughty Stories* as a
> way of encouraging the children to feel comfortable with reading mate-
> rial and for some the reading level is actually too easy for them. But for
> others it is a challenge, it is almost as if they gain some kudos after sitting
> down, reading the same book that somebody who is a lot more able than
> they are is enjoying as well. If you are in a Year 6 class and you had say,
> Each, Peach, Pear, Plum you might open yourself up to some criticism.
> Nobody says that with *Naughty Stories*. It has been OK to look at these
> because it is presented in a different way.
>
> (Sheffield IT co-ordinator)

This kind of equality of access is important for pupils with special educational needs.

> We will make a point of ensuring that children with special needs have
> got access because something like *Naughty Stories* reinforces skills that we
> know they would otherwise find threatening. So children who are reluc-
> tant readers or who have a fear of creative material will quite happily sit
> and use that, and use the hardware appropriately as well. Even if their
> overall skills might be fairly limited, because they want to make the
> computer tell the story they will use it, and they will learn what to do.
> Hopefully, they will learn and they will use it to assist their reading. Even
> though their reading skills are not very good, they can start to learn some
> prediction skills. You can actually see it happening.
>
> (Midlands teacher)

Being able to hear the story and follow the text on the screen therefore
has clear advantages for pupils who experience difficulties with reading. The
layout of the text on the larger and more public computer screen encourages children to talk to each other and the mouse pointer, which is much
thinner than a thumb or finger, makes it easier for children to identify
individual words for each other. Moreover, as Sally McKeown (1995) points

out, CD-ROMs have a lot to offer children who have difficulty with traditional print-based text. Computers can provide a life-line for children with
severe sight problems. The screen is back lit so the text and pictures are illu-
minated to present a clear, high-resolution image. Some children can benefit
from software which offers a range of print sizes while others use a large
monitor which provides a correspondingly bigger image. Similarly CD-ROM
technology can provide hearing-impaired pupils with access to information
in a more immediate and accessible form than was previously possible.

Boys may well benefit more than girls from using the computer to support
their reading. The majority of struggling readers in schools are boys and
working with computers is seen as a high-status, predominantly male, activity.

> Most of the reading undertaken in schools is story reading, and this is
> most often modelled by women infant teachers. It may be that, at a time
> when children are establishing their gender identities, story reading
> becomes associated with feminine behaviour. This is speculation, but it
> seems that any reading technology which is advantageous to boys might
> be a welcome addition to classroom practice.
>
> (Medwell 1996: 45)

While we recognise the potential benefits of talking books over traditional
print-based material, we are aware of the need for multimedia texts for readers of all ages. The novelty of multimedia texts may mean that older pupils
are prepared to tolerate early years material such as *Naughty Stories*. But
we would argue that such material has limited value even for the young
readers for whom it was initially intended. If talking books are to be used
to support reading in primary schools and beyond then we need to see an
increase in the production of high-quality material. Ideally such materials
would reflect the wealth of 'picture books' now available for children and
young people while exploiting to the full the facilities which multimedia and
hypertext offer.

LIMITATIONS OF EXISTING TALKING BOOKS

Having established the benefits of talking books to motivate and support
readers we conclude the chapter with some reflections on the limitations of
existing material and suggestions as to possible improvements both in the
type and quality of the material available.

As we have already said, there are far too few talking books to adequately
support early readers. We look forward to seeing the development of more
first school material. We would also like to see more books which support
older pupils with a wide range of abilities. If multimedia books are to become
an integral part of a school's reading programme, rather than something
which exists as an interesting fringe activity, then there needs to be sufficient
material at different levels to support developing readers of all ages.

As with traditional print-based material, levels of difficulty or reading ages is only one criterion which we need to consider when choosing books for children. Applying what Liz Waterland (1985) calls the 'pleasure principle' should encourage children to enjoy reading and develop a reading habit.

> There is only one criterion that needs to be taken into account when choosing books for any age of child if reading is to be approached as a natural learning activity. Will the child enjoy the book?
>
> (Waterland 1985: 19)

The pleasure principle provides a useful starting point; however, it should not be the teacher's only consideration. In choosing books teachers also have to be guided by notions of quality. They have to encourage children to read books which have artistic, moral or educational value on the grounds that poor-quality books cripple the children's 'imaginative, linguistic or moral powers, as well as their ability to come to grips with and appreciate good quality literature' (Chambers 1983: 102). It is to be hoped that when reviewing talking books, teachers will apply the same criteria they use for traditional print-based material. Teachers will look for high-quality books that children enjoy and which reflect the kind of society that they and their children's parents wish to promote.

Currently the majority of talking books are multimedia adaptations of existing paper-based books and familiarity with the texts should make selection easier. However, not all books translate successfully into the new medium. For example, Mackey (1996) is highly critical of a CD-ROM version of Frances Hodgson Burnett's *The Secret Garden*. She argues that the short film clips and clichéd sound effects do little to add to an appreciation of the original story. Moreover, she argues, computer animations are quickly developing their own conventions and clichés.

> Anything with a possible sound effect is more likely to be accentuated, and the sound effects are already clichés, even in these early days of the medium. You can be certain that anything permitting a scream or a stamping of feet will be given an icon for the mouse to click on.
>
> (Mackey 1996: 15)

Her comments highlight once again the need to think about the use of the technology and the way in which film clips and animations work to enhance or detract from the text.

The attractions of the multi-layered book which has 'new things to think about and new things to appreciate whenever the reader chooses to read it' (Waterland 1992: 35) have long been recognised. Multimedia technology now offers exciting possibilities for talking books which are multi-layered not only in terms of combining text, sound and animation but also in terms of exploiting the possibilities of hypertext. We would like to see talking books written for the new technologies which go beyond the notions of linear narrative. We would take as a model games software such as *The Ultimate Haunted House* in which children are encouraged to explore the different rooms and interact with the weird and wonderful creatures they find there in search of the keys that will help them escape (Figures 3.3 and 3.4). We were impressed with children's engagement with this activity and with the quality of the narratives that they construct within the different rooms. When leaving the kitchen, for example, Emma made a point of turning the oven off again because 'We don't want to start a fire'. When it was suggested that a fire might be a good thing as the house was haunted, she replied, 'Not while I'm still inside'. Imagine the possibilities for parallel stories, character analysis and multiple interpretations which would be created if talking books were written as non-linear and interactive text.

However, with all computer-based activities, the quality of children's learning is dependent, at least in part, on the way the activity is organised and supported by the teacher. As we have shown in this chapter, without appropriate support and direction from the teacher, working with talking books can become a passive activity with little constructive learning.

Figure 3.3 The Ultimate Haunted House provides an example of a non-linear narrative

Figure 3.4 The challenge is to explore the different rooms in *The Ultimate Haunted House* and find the thirteen hidden keys

Our observations also suggest that the use of 'talking book' software can easily be an essentially passive affair, in which children do little more than watch and listen.

(NCET 1996: 9)

The success of talking books to support and motivate reading will always depend in part on the quality of input from teachers and parents.

Acknowledgement

We are grateful to Anna Sewell for her review of current literature and insightful comments, both of which have made an invaluable contribution to our work on reading with multimedia texts.

Chapter 4

Learners and information handling

CD-ROM can be used to store and play back vast amounts of data in the form of text, diagrams, photographs, video and sound. This could have a major impact on the future curriculum by giving learners access to more information, and to more appealingly presented information, than was ever the case in the past. In this chapter we explore the use of encyclopedia discs in developing research strategies and data-handling skills. The importance of these skills is highlighted by the *National Curriculum Orders for English* (DfE 1995) which requires pupils to develop two major and related skills. One of these is searching, selecting and retrieving information. The other is to use the data constructively within the context of the curriculum.

Our work suggests that students appreciate the immediacy and accessibility of encyclopedia software (see for example the report by Collins and her colleagues: NCET 1996).

> Pupils are motivated by the interactive nature of the CDs. There is more scope for information handling with the CDs, whether searching for photos, looking at encyclopedias or using a model.
>
> (London teacher)

In addition, groups of pupils can make good use of CD-ROM encyclopedias, even when given relatively little specific direction or intervention by their teachers. But teachers are aware that to get the most out of the discs, pupils (even the most able) need to be given instruction in planning and carrying out independent research. As the NCET evaluation suggests: 'Children work most effectively when CD-ROM-based activities have clearly defined purposes' (NCET 1996: 12). But what constitutes a 'clearly defined purpose' and how far can (and should) pupils be involved in defining and take some responsibility for their work? How are pupils' research activities constrained or encouraged by the particular software they are using?

We shall address these underlying issues in three distinct but related sections. We begin by identifying the difficulties that teachers face in designing appropriate activities for pupils. By looking at a range of activities, we identify the kinds of tasks that have proved useful in supporting pupils engaged in independent research. Next, we discuss the software itself, the selection of data, and the structure and organisation of the material. We then conclude with a case study which illustrates the issues we have raised by reference to work carried out by a small group of pupils using two pieces of software (*Information Finder* and *Creepy Crawlies*) as part of their class project on insects.

DESIGNING ACTIVITIES FOR YOUNG INFORMATION HANDLERS

In their evaluation of CD-ROMs in secondary schools Steadman and his colleagues (NCET 1992) identify two types of users which they call 'purposeful user' and 'serendipitous browser'. In this chapter we use the term 'purposeful use' to describe activities in which individuals or groups use the technology to find specific information or solve particular problems. Purposeful use may well begin with clearly defined objectives and search strategies, set either by the pupils themselves or by their teacher. On other occasions, the pupils may begin to define the purpose of the search through their engagement with the technology. Whether the pupils are working at home or at school, purposeful use is dependent on there being a learning outcome such as finding new information or refining existing knowledge. An activity is purposeful whenever learning occurs, even if the original objectives are not met. For example, a pupil who uses a multimedia encyclopedia to learn something about the circulatory system would be described as a purposeful user even if the original task was to find the names of the bones in the leg.

In comparison 'browsing' is relatively random and unstructured as pupils flick from screen to screen. Browsing becomes serendipitous only if, and when, the pupils stumble across something which they find interesting and/or informative. Serendipitous browsing can lead to purposeful use when pupils begin by browsing and then go on to identify and pursue an area of interest.

In both the secondary and the primary evaluations there is an implied assumption that browsing should be discouraged in school. Certainly, the benefits of encouraging pupils to become purposeful users is a recurring theme throughout the primary evaluation. The reasons for this are, at least in part, related to the way in which learning is perceived, organised and valued in schools.

Serendipitous browsing may indeed be a common use of CD-ROMs in homes where individuals have almost unlimited access to the technology and no restraints on developing their own particular interests. Moreover, there is no pressure on individuals to show that their time has been used effectively by demonstrating what they have learned and relating it to a predetermined curriculum. In schools, however, pupils work within a number of constraints that discourage serendipitous browsing. They have limited access; at best they may have to share a CD-ROM system with thirty or more other pupils.

They are likely to work in small groups with peers who may have very different interests, skills and experiences. This will make collaboration difficult unless the group is able to establish and maintain a shared focus for its work. In our experience it is invariably the teacher who provides this shared focus. The teacher is seen as having authority over the activity and may be asked to adjudicate during disputes between pupils. In addition, pupils and teachers in schools have to work within curriculum constraints. They are also expected to demonstrate the relevance of what is learned to predetermined topics or subjects. Unfortunately, all these constraints can prevent pupils from taking control of their learning. They leave little time for serendipitous browsing. Given these pressures it is not surprising that there is such an emphasis on enabling pupils to become purposeful users of the technology.

However, as we show in the following case studies, purposeful use is often prefaced by short bursts of serendipitous browsing. It could be argued that one of the strengths of multimedia technology is its potential for supporting pupils as independent learners. If this is so, then the task for the teacher is to empower pupils to set their own agendas and find answers to their own questions.

All this suggests a number of factors that have to be borne in mind when designing CD-ROM-based activities. Are activities aimed towards serendipitous browsing or purposeful use? Are they primarily pupil-centred or teacher-directed? Irrespective of where the activity fits on these continua, pupils need to develop their skills in searching, selecting and retrieving information. They also need to be able to use the data constructively within the context of the curriculum.

In fact, the teachers to whom we spoke thought that pupils needed to be taught research and data-handling skills if they were to make good use of CD-ROM encyclopedias (for a fuller discussion see NCET 1996: 16–17). We also found that teachers were uncertain how to set appropriate activities for pupils to carry out.

Most teachers find it relatively easy to devise simple introductory activities for pupils. In schools highlighted by the NCET primary evaluation, even relatively inexperienced pupils (as young as 5) were successful in achieving the tasks set by their teacher. A particularly effective example of such a lesson was one in which pupils were asked to work in pairs to find a picture of a railway train and print it out. Here the aim was to engage the pupils in the process of searching the CD-ROM for information. By the end of the lesson the whole class had successfully located relevant information and printed out pictures. They 'had no great difficulty with the task, in fact they were delighted with the pictures they produced and carried them proudly back to the classroom' (NCET 1996: 11). As an introductory activity the lesson worked extremely well because it had clearly defined and attainable aims. Moreover, success in completing the task was not dependent on prior knowledge of the subject or familiarity with the technology.

Lessons such as this have an important role in familiarising pupils with the various search strategies available. However, as with learning the alphabet when using traditional print-based encyclopedias, this is only a first step in teaching pupils to carry out independent research. The next step is to encourage pupils to use information constructively. Setting aside the notion of who establishes the agenda, there is an assumption that the pupils need to have a 'clear research question in mind at the start' (NCET 1992). However, teachers should take care to ensure that the research questions are neither too closed nor unstructured.

Open and closed questions

Closed questions may lead to unsuccessful searches either because the information is not available or because certain prior knowledge is needed. For example, one group of pupils were unable to answer the question 'Where do mosquitoes live?' because the information was not held on the database. They had to consult a further piece of software to find the answer. Another group of pupils became increasingly frustrated when their searches failed to reveal the name of 'the world's tallest building'. The pupils tried a number of 'key words' but without success. It was only when one of them remembered which country had the world's tallest building that they were able to access information about that country and find the answer. Clearly, without this specific prior knowledge the pupils would not have succeeded.

At the other end of the continuum, completely open-ended research questions can prevent pupils from moving from serendipitous browsing into purposeful use. For example, when a group of 9 year olds were sent to find out about 'bridges' they found appropriate text (through the search facility) but were then unable to select information which they thought would be relevant to the class topic. They occupied the rest of their 'computer time' copying a list of seven types of bridges. Another group of older pupils were given a similar problem. They were asked 'to find out about the Second World War and produce something for their topic folder'. The pupils' prior knowledge and obvious fascination for the subject made their search seem relatively meaningful. However, their lack of focus or search strategies meant that they had little to contribute to their topic folders. These examples suggest that children need appropriate research strategies if they are to make the most of the encyclopedia-type software.

But where to begin? It is important to work with pupils from the start to decide on appropriate research questions. These questions have to define an area for study while still leaving opportunities for a wide range of acceptable information or answers. For example, 'the Second World War' is too large and wide ranging a subject and needs to be broken down into smaller, more manageable topics such as 'specific battles', 'kinds of weapons used' or 'biographies of key protagonists'. Similarly, pupils may find studying 'The Victorians' extremely daunting but be quite able to find out about 'a Victorian invention' or 'Victorian schools'. These topic areas could be generated through discussion or brainstorming exercises where the teacher works with small groups or the whole class. The extent to which pupils are able to define research areas for themselves will, of course, depend on their age and experience in carrying out independent research. It would also depend on the pupils' prior knowledge and interests. Pupils who are carrying out their own research are more likely to be able to identify what they need to know and be motivated to find the answers than pupils who are completing teacher-directed tasks.

We suggest that structured but open-ended research questions are the most effective means of supporting pupils' exploration of CD-ROM encyclopedias.

> It is easy to set 'open-ended' tasks that leave even the most conscientious children marooned and frustrated in a tangle of information, with only a limited sense of how to navigate their way out, and such software does not always provide them with enough help in re-orientation. On the other hand, for children who are content simply to flick from one screen to the next without any particular search strategy, the same disk may offer no more than a stimulating but superficial pattern of novelty and movement.
> (NCET 1996: 16)

Structured but open-ended questions provide enough guidance to enable pupils to identify relevant or useful information without predetermining exactly what that information should be. Giving pupils freedom within a structure is extremely important in enabling them to become truly independent learners. Having that freedom opens the possibility that they will not find the required information on the CD-ROM they have been given and may require them to consult other sources including new or unfamiliar software. This raises the general question of how we can set about assessing the value of new titles.

ISSUES IN EVALUATING ENCYCLOPEDIA SOFTWARE

Here we look at some of the considerations, many of which re-emerge in a general context in Chapter 5, for evaluating encyclopedia software. These are representation and selection of data, the ability to play with text and the use and organisation of the different media. Obviously there are other more technical questions to consider (e.g. Will it run on my machine?) in choosing software (see NCET 1994a: 239–40).

Representation and selection of information

The value of CD-ROM technology cannot be divorced from the data on the discs. We reported earlier that much of the encyclopedia-type software currently available on CD-ROM in the UK is American rather than British in its language and cultural perspective (NCET 1992, 1996) and this does concern some teachers. Worries have also been expressed about a gender imbalance in some of the software. For example, one teacher reported to Collins and her colleagues that pupils in their class had

> noticed a male bias in the encyclopaedia that they were using. They found that there was more on Pierre Curie than Madame Curie, they found that there was no information on the contribution that women made during the Second World War, and they noticed that accompanying pictures and general information were always of men.
>
> (NCET 1996: 15)

Of course this is not a new problem and in this case the teacher made use of this opportunity to discuss male-centred approaches to history with the class. However, as the report by Steadman and his colleagues (NCET 1992) points out, there is a need to 'reawaken sensitivities' to gender or racial bias for the advent of CD-ROM.

Teachers are also concerned at the accessibility of the text. This is an obvious issue for younger or less able pupils where there is a shortage of encyclopedia-type software with simple text, but it is also a general problem, as some secondary teachers reporting on the use of *Encarta* with their students told us. Clearly, the pupils' interest in the information on the disc is awakened by language they can understand. Pupils are extremely selective in their reading of text and simply ignore that which is too difficult for them.

In the UK teachers want to develop ways of using CD-ROM systems to support the National Curriculum and feel that software manufacturers generally do not reflect the significance of the National Curriculum in the design of their titles.

Some teachers want specially designed National Curriculum software. Others feel that the most important thing is to focus on underlying skills rather than the content of the National Curriculum *per se*. The former approach points away from the general encyclopedia disc, either towards more sophisticated variants of the simulations already available on floppy disks, or towards the equally familiar CAL (computer-assisted learning) packages in which some part of the 'teaching' is done through the software. There is a challenge here for software houses to develop UK-based materials which have a tighter curriculum fit but still cater for exploratory learning styles which CD-ROM supports so well.

Playing with text

Software design is a crucial factor in determining the levels and nature of pupils' interaction with the material being presented. Specifically the existence of notebook facilities on some CD-ROM encyclopedias helps to promote both high levels of pupil interaction and what teachers regard as purposeful use of the technology. These facilities enable pupils to cut and paste text from the encyclopedias. Pupils can then use the text as the basis for their own work. But this indicates a (growing?) need for pupils to have basic word processing skills, so that they can edit the text, and writing skills, so that they know more about taking notes and drafting their work. In this way they would spend less time at the computer worrying about small details of presentation which could be left to later drafts. Without the necessary writing and word processing skills there is an obvious danger that pupils will resort to merely copying the text from an article and passing it off as their own.

Use and organisation of the different media

CD-ROM encyclopedias differ from their print-based predecessors in two distinct ways: the range of media used and their complex underlying, often opaque, organisational structure. Paradoxically, this makes them both more accessible and more difficult to use.

The potential for CD-ROM encyclopedias to incorporate video and sound with the more traditional media text and pictures makes them extremely accessible and attractive, especially to younger learners.

> Pupils that wouldn't be motivated by the idea of research or something in a book, if you say they can look it up on the CD-ROM they get very excited about it.
>
> (Midlands teacher)

Some primary school pupils with whom we worked were surprisingly fascinated by even poor quality animations. We were surprised, for example, to hear pupils talking about how video clips on *Creepy Crawlies* 'showed how the animals moved'. By comparison, we were uninspired by these small, often blurred images and we thought them extremely limited, especially when compared with the superb quality film available in most wildlife programmes. We feel that the early CD-ROMs have a certain novelty value and suspect that the technology will have to improve somewhat if it is going to remain attractive to youngsters who are, after all, growing up in the video age.

Some video clips may be disappointing, but there was wide-scale approval from teachers for sound-tracks, especially those that verbalised the written text (a point we return to in Chapter 6). Teachers felt that these were particularly valuable because they could be used to support poor or less confident readers. Indeed, the majority of teachers interviewed strongly supported CD-ROM use by lower-achieving pupils, especially those with weaker language skills: 'As long as children can click on a mouse they can use the CD-ROM' (Yorkshire teacher).

The range of media help make CD-ROM encyclopedias more attractive and accessible than print-based books. Moreover, the hot spots which link different material together create the possibility for exciting multi-layered, non-linear text in which the 'readers' can navigate their own way through the information. For teachers and pupils this presents a mixed blessing. Vast amounts of information are easily accessible, but navigating your way through this information can be difficult, as one pupil found out.

> Sometimes you get lost in it by pressing the wrong button, but the more you go wrong the further the program goes, so you get really lost in it.
>
> (NCET 1996: 16)

Navigation is made easier where the underlying structure of the software is self-evident and/or logically organised. Two different approaches to the organisation of information is reflected in the following evaluations of *Creepy Crawlies* and *Information Finder*.

Creepy Crawlies may well have been produced for the home market rather than as educational software. The structure of the software appears to encourage serendipitous browsing rather than purposeful use. The disc shows seventy-four animals. For each animal there is written description in English or French, an audio description, a photograph, a family tree and a short video clip. Our main criticism of this software is that it fails to organise the

Figure 4.1 In *Creepy Crawlies* the information is organised around seven themes or categories

seventy-four animals in a way that reflects any kind of hierarchical classification or logical search strategy. The introduction mentions the difference between higher- and lower-order animals but this distinction is not reflected either in the choice of animals or in the way they are classified. The seven organisational categories have no logical structure which means it is not immediately obvious where to look for information about specific animals (Figure 4.1). For example, as one group of pupils pointed out, the mosquito was classified under 'pests' but could well have been classified under 'on the wing' or, given that it may carry deadly diseases, 'killers'.

By comparison, *Information Finder*, an encyclopedia designed for the upper primary and secondary age range, is organised according to hierarchical classifications. Nevertheless, the existence and nature of these classifications may not be obvious to inexperienced learners. Pupils benefit from being taught about the structure of the software and how to navigate through it. *Information Finder* provides 17,000 written articles organised into a series of topics and sub-topics. It also provides maps, pictures and tables. Each article appears side by side with its outline, which gives the user an instant picture of its content and a quick way to select items to view (Figure 4.2). The integrated dictionary allows users to look up any words they do not understand. Gallery, as the name implies, provides quick access to all available pictures

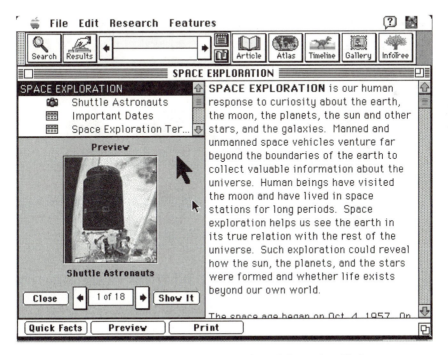

Figure 4.2 A written article with illustrations from *Information Finder*

(Figure 4.3). These are arranged in themes which, unfortunately, seem to bear little or no relation to the topics or themes used to organise the articles. Despite this inconsistency *Information Finder* is an excellent general reference resource which has general applicability within many National Curriculum subject areas.

The comparison between the two discs raises some general issues of organisation of material. Is there a logical structure of material? Is there a hierarchical order? Are the different media organised coherently?

The following case study brings together and develops the themes of this chapter by examining the way in which software design and the need for appropriate research questions both contribute to pupils' exploration of CD-ROM-based encyclopedias.

INSECTS: AN ILLUSTRATIVE CASE STUDY

The three pupils who feature in this case study were from a vertically grouped Year 3/4 class. They were all bright and articulate and all had a reading age above their chronological age. Their experiences of IT had involved the use of the library-based CD-ROM for reference purposes and the use of a classroom-based Archimedes and BBC Master. They had some experience of

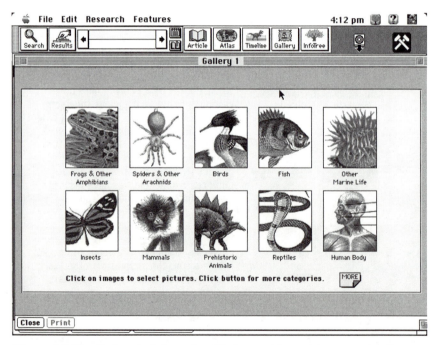

Figure 4.3 The Gallery in *Information Finder* provides quick access to all available pictures

writing and redrafting work on a word processor. The activities discussed here were part of a topic on insects. Before the pupils started work on the CD-ROM they took part in a class lesson on classification.

The case study focuses on two separate episodes, the first while they were using *Creepy Crawlies*, the second when they were using *Information Finder*. The two episodes follow a similar pattern and both lasted about an hour. During both episodes the pupils worked in the library with a 'more experienced' child or 'peer tutor' always on hand to provide technical support and information about search strategies.

Both episodes began with the pupils being given a number of clear but open-ended research questions. Essentially they were asked to

- choose an insect which they thought would be interesting
- find out as much as they could about the insect
- present their findings as a wall display.

Despite the common starting point the two episodes produced extremely different outcomes. When using *Creepy Crawlies* the pupils found it difficult to stay 'on task'. They engaged in random rather than serendipitous browsing and, while they printed out some information, they appeared to learn little from the experience. By comparison, when working with *Information Finder* the same pupils remained 'on task' for the whole hour. They searched the database for interesting facts which they pasted or rewrote into the notebook which formed the basis of their written presentation. The pupils also printed out pictures to illustrate their work.

Episode 1: *Creepy Crawlies*

The pupils began by identifying the alphabetical index as a useful starting point. As they flicked through the list they read out the names of the animals. They appeared to choose animals they had heard of or those with strange and/or exciting sounding names. They made no distinction between insects and higher-order animals and they mispronounced several of the names. They were clearly anxious to choose an insect and in their impatience they did not allow themselves time to read the whole list. This made us wonder if we should have highlighted the benefits of browsing through the database before the pupils began work.

HELEN   (*reading the index*) Mosquito.
DAVID   Yeah, yeah, everyone said the picture was really nice.
HELEN   Mosquito.
DAVID   Can we do the mosquito then?
HELEN   (*laughs*) We've got to see it first before we decide whether we want it (*clicks on mosquito to produce information and picture: Figure 4.4*).
DAVID   We want it, we want it.
HELEN   We want it.

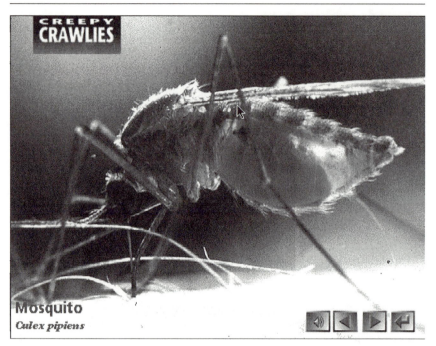

Figure 4.4 Creepy Crawlies *provides accessible pictures of a wide range of creatures*

Having been excited by the idea of studying mosquitoes, the pupils recognise the need to check that this was an insect. They did this by referring to the family tree which appears with every animal.

SUSAN   Yeah, but no, wait a minute, is it an insect?
        (*children check with the classification tree to see if it is an 'Insecta'*)
ALL   Yes.

The pupils were initially excited about their choice of insect and David had some prior knowledge of mosquitoes. Unfortunately, the other pupils were too preoccupied to hear what he had to say.

(*The two girls are reading the text and operating the computer.*)
DAVID   (*in an exaggerated voice*) Mosquito, a mosquito.
SUSAN   Oh. Mosquitoes can kill.
HELEN   Shall I click on mosquito?
SUSAN   Yeah.
DAVID   On a children's wildlife programme once, I saw, mosquitoes have killed. . . . They are the most dangerous animals in the world. Mosquitoes have killed more people than any other.
(*The girls are not really listening to him. They are concentrating on operating the computer.*)

DAVID   What happened?
SUSAN   No, no. What you do is
HELEN   What have you done?
DAVID   You've killed us!
        I saw this wildlife programme once that mosquitoes killed more
        people than any other animal in the world.

They watched the mosquito video a few times and made half-hearted attempts
to sketch the mosquito from the picture. Despite their initial interest and
David's prior knowledge their interest soon flagged. They printed out the
page of information and without reading either the screen or hard copy they
resorted to random browsing of the database.

DAVID   I know what it is, I know what's happened. We can see loads of
        pictures here.
HELEN   Ooh. That's a poisoned dart frog.
SARAH   Yeah.
(*Children become interested and animated in rather a flippant way.*)
DAVID   Oh, we can see loads of pictures. Isn't that one good?
HELEN   I saw that on *Blue Peter*.
DAVID   Ooh that's nice. Thaaat's nice (*being silly*).
HELEN   I love snakes. That's a spitting cobra I think.
DAVID   A huge snake.
(*A lot of laughing and giggling.*)

This could have been a worthwhile data-handling activity. The children had
a task they were motivated to undertake and which they could refine between
them. The software encouraged them (David in particular) to bring in existing
knowledge from other sources into the discussion. But despite the initial
interest in the mosquito video the activity broke down. Why is this? In part
it is because the children are not able to value each other's knowledge (they
do not pick up on David's reference to wildlife programmes or Helen's to
Blue Peter). In part it is because there is no one who can bring the focus
back to the research question. But there is also a problem with the software.
They seem distracted by the wealth of information on offer and have difficulty seeing how it is organised. Immediately after this episode one of the
pupils summarised their experience of using *Creepy Crawlies*:

> *Creepy Crawlies* was fun but it wasn't interesting. If you had a long time
> for the *Creepy Crawlies* and you weren't looking for something in partic-
> ular, you could have a lot of fun just sort of looking around and having
> a look at the pictures close up, seeing the films, reading bits of informa-
> tion here and there. We could have an awful lot of fun. But if you're
> looking for something particular and it's a particular topic like we're doing,
> it doesn't show that much information.
>
> (David)

The fact that this software offers sound and video makes it a popular choice for many pupils as a piece of entertainment. However, as the episode above demonstrated, it may have limited value as a piece of educational software.

Episode 2: *Information Finder*

By comparison, the following episode shows the same group of pupils engaging with text and consequently learning a lot about the insect of their choice. Directed by the pupil tutor, the pupils began their search through an examination of the gallery which gives them easy access to all the pictures on the encyclopedia. As with *Creepy Crawlies* they made their choice from the first half of the alphabetical list. Having found a picture they liked, they then found the related article. They did this by going through the hierarchically structured 'info tree'. They had obviously not realised the direct link between the pictures in 'gallery' and the articles. Their approach seemed awkward and time consuming but, perhaps because they did not know a better way, they did not seem to mind.

DAVID	That's interesting.
HELEN	I like that one (*referring to a picture of the life cycle of a bed bug*); they are all different.
DAVID	It's small, little.
RICHARD	Is that why our parents say don't let the bed bugs bite, or something like that (*laughs – pointing at screen*)?
DAVID	Why?
DAVID HELEN	(*Muttering while reading the text*)
DAVID	That sounds interesting.
HELEN	Yeah, it does.
DAVID	Yep, we'll do this.
HELEN	Wait.
RICHARD	Wow, it feeds on blood.
HELEN	It pierces the skin of its victim and then it sucks up the blood. It bites. Its bites cause the skin of some people to swell and itch.
ADAM	So do you want to do that one?
ALL	Yeah (*all smiling and looking excited*).

Having decided that bed bugs looked interesting they began reading the text on the screen. The fact that they read this text but not the *Creepy Crawlies* text is interesting, especially as the article in *Information Finder* is both longer and in a smaller font. While they read, they select relevant information.

DAVID	That's an interesting bit. 'Bed bugs usually hide in the day and hunt for food at night.'

HELEN	Yeah and look. 'They hide in mattresses and bedsprings, between floorboards, or in cracks in plaster.'
DAVID	Yeah, let's put that down as a fact.
ADAM	OK, so you want to highlight this.
	(*Children reading silently, David using the mouse.*)
ADAM	'250 eggs hatch in about one or two days.'
DAVID	Now we want to put that down, don't we, in our notepad?

Perhaps the existence of a cut and paste facility in this software helped pupils to focus on the available information and select that which seemed most interesting or relevant. The notebook or notepad certainly seemed to be a major factor in encouraging pupil involvement.

DAVID	Hang on (*leaning towards screen*). Yeah, that looks like a good beginning bit.
HELEN RICHARD }	Yeah.
HELEN	Yes, we want to put all that (*indicating the text on the screen*).
DAVID	OK, so let's.
ADAM	You want to click there. Go up there (*pause while David positions the cursor and clicks*). Press the apple (*Helen presses the key*) and the C.
DAVID	Apple and C at the same time.
HELEN RICHARD }	(*look down at keyboard*)
ADAM	Now press notepad – that's notepad.

Having used the notepad, the pupils were able to reflect on what they had done and to offer some advice for other pupils.

DAVID	Perhaps you should collect quite a lot of information before you keep, before you go to the notepad because we had to go to the notepad, back to the disc, then back to the notepad, all the time.
HELEN	Then it's good to like write things in yourself as well.
DAVID	Don't just copy and highlight everything from the information. It's better to write, it was actually more fun in the end when we wrote it.

In this episode the children work well as a group. They seem to listen to each other and are able to reach a consensus based on a shared interest in bed bugs. At one point Richard brings in something he already knows ('Is that why our parents say don't let the bed bugs bite?') which David comments on and which leads to further inquiry. The children are able to access and select their information they want for the notepad and produce their own text and, in the words of Douglas Barnes (1979), 'make the knowledge their own'. Given that this was the same group of children as earlier, the episode shows that the design of the software, in particular the existence of a notepad, can be crucial. The children still have technical hurdles; they use time-consuming and clumsy procedures for cutting and pasting text; they do not access the 'info tree' in the easiest way but they are able to work through these difficulties. However, the software will be exploited only if it is used to support more open-ended tasks and if children in the group have the maturity to work together.

IMPLICATIONS FOR CLASSROOM PRACTICE

The major point of this chapter is that teachers, pupils and software designers share a responsibility for developing multimedia information-handling skills. Effective use of multimedia texts involves the identification of clearly defined but at the same time open-ended tasks. Such tasks help to guide the pupil through the wealth of available data without predetermining what consti-tutes relevant or interesting information. Ideally, pupils would be encouraged to take an increasingly active role in the whole process as they become expe-rienced information handlers and more knowledgeable about the subjects being researched. This shift from teacher-centred to more pupil-directed tasks involves identifying the skills and processes involved and making these explicit to pupils. What are these skills and processes? Fundamental is that students can refine research questions, access information and assess its relevance for their inquiry. This takes in computer skills, such as being able to search a database and knowing how to cut and paste text, writing skills, such as drafting and editing text, and social skills such as working co-operatively within a group.

Pupil-directed learning necessitates a change in pupil–teacher relationships with the teacher increasingly assuming the role of facilitator and guide. This raises the issue of teacher authority, which goes beyond important and sensi-tive issues of classroom discipline.

> When pupils are encouraged to ask questions, invariably they will raise subjects beyond the expertise of the teacher. Teachers are no longer able to maintain an image of themselves as the custodians of all knowledge.
>
> (Collins 1996: 192)

Teachers and pupils also have to learn to deal with the fact that pupils may well raise difficult and/or unanswerable questions. This can feel threatening especially to pupils accustomed to being spoon-fed by teachers offering digestible morsels of information.

In this chapter we have seen that notebook facilities have an important role to play in encouraging pupils to engage with materials (text and pictures) which they can cut and paste into their own work. There is no doubt that word processing can radically improve presentation. Typed text looks neat and is more likely to be revised and edited than text which has to be laboriously copied out each time a change is made. Moreover, incorporating existing material from multimedia encyclopedias can lead to interesting discussions about different writing styles and audiences.

However, the existence of notebook facilities accentuates the difficulties that pupils often experience when asked to carry out independent research. The process of identifying relevant information and note-taking are highly complex skills, and pupils who are not trained to develop these skills often resort to lifting chunks of text into their own writing without understanding the material they are using. As we saw in the *Creepy Crawlies* example, pupils can print out pages of text without even reading them or considering the relevance of the material. As with traditional print-based materials, this wholesale copying of text has to be discouraged as it does little to enhance pupils' understanding, not to mention possible copyright implications. For notebooks to be effective, pupils have to be taught how to extract information and make it their own.

Chapter 5

The medium and the message
Learners and the words, sounds and images of multimedia

In Chapters 3 and 4 we looked at reading and information handling with multimedia. Here our attention shifts to more general considerations of teaching and learning with multimedia, illustrated within a variety of settings. The introduction of multimedia into schools is leading to a change of focus from content-free to content-rich or 'content-heavy' programmes. That change creates a challenge for researchers, teachers and students to learn to examine the selection and presentation of text, sound and images and their contribution to learning.

This chapter, which examines the words, sounds and images presented to learners by multimedia, has a more exploratory feel than the others – reflecting the newness of the field and the lack of an existing literature which draws together both pedagogical and cultural concerns in the context of multimedia. We realise that the study of images is not a new field *per se*. For example, writers such as John Berger (1972) and others have analysed signs, others have sensitised us to the way we look at photographs and at art; some authors (e.g. Buckingham 1993) have discussed the sometimes surprising ways in which young people watch television. There is also a literature which looks at the use of images in textbooks. The challenge is to find a way of using these concepts and applying them with a particular focus on the concerns of classroom teachers using multimedia software.

First, we distinguish two closely related themes or areas: the role and value of images in learning and the portrayals and representations made by the images used in multimedia. Then we move to specific examples of multimedia which use images (sounds, animations, photographs, video) either to enhance learning, or to represent concepts (in the case of science), people or other cultures and countries. Here we include views and comments from teachers and pupils responding to the examples they see and hear. We discuss the idea of 'critical media literacy' and suggest practical ideas and frameworks which can be used by teachers and students in looking critically at the words and images of multimedia products. Finally we look briefly at the way that knowledge is increasingly being packaged and computerised into multimedia systems and the consequences this has for learning.

IMAGES AND LEARNING: VALUE ADDED AND VALUE TAKEN AWAY?

The first area concerns the importance for learning of the visual images used in multimedia. What impact and influence do the images used on discs have? Their chief benefit is that they offer a more direct and accessible means of communication than printed text. For many children learning to decode print can be time consuming and frustrating; even fluent readers may find text dense and at times impenetrable. Even when they can read it, there may still be a problem with understanding it, especially when it includes difficult and abstract concepts.

Images often help a pupil to learn a new concept or idea. Animations may help a concept to 'come alive' or gain meaning for a learner. But are there also difficulties in the use of images for learning?

One important issue is the extent to which 'mental imagery', and the demand on the user's imagination, is taken away if the image is presented on the screen. Providing a concrete representation of a character or an event on screen may inhibit or even conflict with the user's imagination of the sound or image. Is, for example, watching a television or film version of a novel such as *Pride and Prejudice* the same as reading the book? Does listening to a radio version of *The Hitch Hiker's Guide to the Galaxy* detract from the need to conjure up images when reading Adams's book? It could also be argued (as the Bullock Report 1975 on language in the curriculum did) that subject teaching in secondary schools, e.g. science, should not be trying to avoid, or find ways around, the activity of engaging pupils in reading. Is the use of sound to 'read aloud' text counter-productive in developing reading skills? Is it a 'cop-out'?

But to see images as *opposed* to text is to misunderstand multimedia. We need to examine the interaction of images, sounds and written words in learning – the link between what is heard and what is seen. For example, in Chapter 4 we saw how playing back the recording of a sentence might assist children in learning to read. But should the reading always be a straight rendition of the written text? A word for word spoken version may help a poor reader, but this feature of a disc will not help to overcome conceptual barriers for a learner. For example, *Earth and Universe* contains a section on the tides, a notoriously difficult event to explain fully and clearly. Text appears on the screen and the user can choose the option of hearing that text read aloud. But this in no way helps to make the explanation any clearer or less conceptually demanding.

Just as in textbooks and worksheets, the reading age or 'readability' of written text on multimedia screens needs to be examined and checked. We cannot assume that the addition of a spoken version of the written text increases readability, enhances understanding or overcomes conceptual barriers. (Incidentally, the text which appears on multimedia screens needs to be proof-read and spell-checked – some multimedia designers take much less care with written text than would be taken by a book publisher. It is almost as if the presence of several media reduces the importance of ensuring that the written words on the screen are correct and clear.

REPRESENTATION AND UNDER-REPRESENTATION

Those responsible for producing a multimedia application have made certain choices and selections for pictures, diagrams, animation, video, written text and spoken text. How were these choices made and on what basis? Unlike a book, it is often difficult to see clearly who the authors of a multimedia product are. It is almost as if authorship and ownership get lost. In judging a book we often look at the author's credentials and background. This is less transparent with multimedia and its teams of 'producers'. There is a consequent danger that multimedia will present itself as the 'truth' rather than the truth according to a certain author or authors.

People, events, ideas and concepts are portrayed in the photographs, animations and video clips of multimedia. How well represented are different groups, e.g. women or black people? Are images of certain groups seen only in certain contexts, e.g. black athletes and women models? How are women and men portrayed on the screen? Who is doing what – for example, in a sports science disc is the man shown as the footballer and the woman as the tennis player?

In Chapter 4 we described a reported male bias in an encyclopedia disc that children were using (p. 50). This raises the question: will a disc with such under-representation 'appeal' more to a male or female learner? Should it be used in the classroom? (It is worth noting that the teacher in this study made use of the children's observations of the disc to discuss male-centred approaches to history with the children. Reference could perhaps be made to the feminist term 'herstory', used by some writers as a counterbalance to 'history'.)

We also need to consider the cultural features of multimedia, which are often more implicit (and less obvious) in books than in multimedia:

> All teaching materials that deal in any way with images of the world bring with them a set of attitudes and assumptions, explicit or implicit, conscious or unconscious, which are based on broader cultural perspectives.
>
> (Hicks 1980: 3)

Likewise, every multimedia application has certain cultural features. We have mentioned visual images, but voices are certainly not culturally neutral. The voices for a spoken presentation have been selected by someone: are the voices male or female? 'Experts' are often used as presenters on a disc, e.g. Patrick Moore, Helen Sharman, particularly for science. If so, why, and what messages do they convey? Are a variety of accents and dialects included, representing different classes – or is the spoken output purely 'neutral standard

English'? Many discs are imported from the USA . Do American voices, e.g. on *A to Zap* for early learners or *The Ultimate Human Body* for older learners, have any impact on or reaction from learners in other countries?

Children to whom we have spoken seem occasionally amused but totally unconcerned by the use of American accents or 'expert' voices, perhaps because they are experienced television watchers. It seems to be more of a concern for teachers (who sometimes worry about American pronunciations and spellings), for curriculum 'leaders' such as Nicholas Tate of the School Curriculum and Assessment Authority (SCAA) or politicians who lament the erosion of 'English Culture'.

In the same context, how authentic are portrayals of foreign countries on discs, e.g. are the French all white, croissant eaters and wine drinkers? How glossy are the images presented of (say) French life? How are they selected and on what grounds (e.g. pedagogical, cultural)? Can multimedia bring a culture into the classroom even if it is just somebody's selection of that culture? This again is something we look at when we consider specific examples of discs in use.

One issue here is the use of music and colour and their dependence on a culture. Henderson (1993: 165) concludes that 'IMM (interactive multimedia) courseware can never be culturally neutral'. She describes her research with Australian Torres Strait islanders which recognised the importance of colour and music:

> The courseware developer/designer had to be able to step aside from Western colour preferences and recognise that numerous bright colours on the screen help Torres Strait Islanders distinguish among key elements and cause them absolutely no aesthetic discomfort. A multi-sensory approach which includes culturally specific music, language and images was also found to provide motivation to remain on-task. Utilising the music, pictures and first language of the students' culture is not cosmetic or an act of tokenism. Pedagogically, such elements acknowledge the students' identity in the learning task. In the words of one of the students, these features are 'familiar and relaxing; they lessen the tensions in learning'. The use of voice – in English and the students' first language – allows the lecturer to personalise explanations or express information in ways different from the text on the screen. One student said, 'It makes what is being presented real'.
>
> (Henderson 1993: 165–6)

Thus our main concern in this area is the filtering, packaging and representation of 'knowledge' in multimedia. Textbook writers have for a long time been portraying and encapsulating subject matter in a textbook format. Authors and editors have been making critical decisions about the text, pictures, diagrams and other representations of their subject matter which are to be included in the final product. In a sense they act as filters by distilling out knowledge in areas such as science and the humanities and re-presenting it in a new package. Teachers also play a key part in this filtering and re-presentation when they use textbooks and other resources. The same decisions affect the makers and the users of multimedia, with added impor-tance due to the additional media (sound, animation, video) conferring more motivation, charisma, glamour and authority on the final representation. Their importance is further increased by the fact that multimedia systems are more likely to be used independently of the teacher.

The crucial point is that CD-ROM users construct meaning from what CD-ROM producers and authors have chosen to package and present. We need to examine critically how the knowledge they present is selected, constructed, filtered and packaged – and to teach students to do this. We can also pose the question: which of these issues does multimedia share with textbooks and other print and paper resources – and which are unique to multimedia with its capacity for animation, sound, video and interactivity? We shall discuss ideas for developing a critical outlook and awareness in using multimedia – a kind of 'critical media literacy' – and touch upon the idea of 'visual literacy'. But first we consider some examples.

CASE STUDIES OF MULTIMEDIA IN EDUCATION

We have chosen some examples of multimedia currently in use in school education with a variety of age groups from different subject areas, but these do not provide an exhaustive coverage of the curriculum or of different phases of education.

We use the idea of *access* to provide a framework for the varied examples of discs below: the effective use of multimedia in education can increase and extend access to learning, for different age groups and different abilities. For example, access to literature, stories and story telling, access to processes, concepts and experiments, and access to other people, cultures and experi-ences, all can be enhanced by the images, sounds and animation of multimedia. Our theme of access is largely a positive one, but we also look briefly at possible difficulties associated with using images.

Access to literature, stories and story telling

The three examples here illustrate ways in which multimedia can engage young people in stories and story telling.

Animations within talking books

In Chapter 3 we saw how hot spots within the *The Tortoise and the Hare* added to children's understanding of the story. This was illustrated further when we compared children talking about the books they had had read to them with the talking books they experienced on the computer. The comparison shows the stimulus that the talking books gave to children's talk and the greater understanding of the role of the story teller. Here Stephen and Kylie talk about the story they had had read to them:

INTERVIEWER What was the story about?
STEPHEN He was fast and the tortoise was slow and the tortoise could do things more often than the hare.
KYLIE The tortoise won, the tortoise was slow ... the hare was winning at first and he fell asleep and he let the tortoise go past him.
INTERVIEWER What else do you remember?
KYLIE Nothing.

(In fact both go on to respond to factual questions such as 'What happened to the hare?', 'What happened to the tortoise?', with short answers.

Here the same two children are talking about the *Living Book* (see Figure 5.1).

INTERVIEWER What happened in the story this time?
STEPHEN Well, at the beginning the stork was sitting in the chair and he said I'm going to tell you the story of this person ...

Figure 5.1 Living Books such as *The Tortoise and the Hare* can add to children's understanding and stimulate talk

	and he read it to us . . . and after he read a little bit of the story you could do things, like the horses and people and stuff and you could change the pages.
KYLIE	You know this woman, she was in a window, she said everyone come in and join the fun.
STEPHEN	And then she popped back into the window and you could change the pages.
KYLIE	I pointed at the door and there was a bang, bang of guitars . . . I can't think of anything else.
INTERVIEWER	What happened to the hare?
KYLIE	He fell asleep, I saw him lying down asleep . . . fast asleep . . . I don't know what happened.
STEPHEN	Because the hare was too lazy to carry on, he had a little rest and he fell asleep.
KYLIE	He kept running . . . he wanted to win, he wanted to keep running, the hare was having a little rest . . . he kept running, the hare woke up and saw him, rushed, jumped across the finish line but the tortoise already won.

In our view, the comparison shows the stimulus that the *Living Book* gave to the children's talk. In the second interview Stephen is not simply answering questions, he is telling a story. He begins by reminding us that this is a story within a story, i.e. one told by the stork. His style is that of a narrator: 'Well, at the beginning the stork was sitting in the chair'. Both children then mix the story of *The Tortoise and the Hare* with some of the on-screen interaction: 'I pointed at the door and there was a bang, bang of guitars'. Kylie then ends the story with a flourish. When talking, both children have been acting out gestures and movements from the story. For example, as Kylie says: 'He kept running . . . he wanted to win, he wanted to keep running', she is moving her arms in imitation of a runner.

Macbeth: an integration of text and moving image?

The CD-ROM *Macbeth* (HarperCollins) contains screens showing Shakespeare's text alongside short video clips from a production of the play (Figure 5.2). The written text, which users can follow as the video proceeds, is made more accessible by hot spots which learners can click on to explain the meaning of obscure or difficult words. The presentation begins with a short blast of music and a backdrop which sets the scene for the play.

The combination of pictures, video, music and text combine to make Shakespeare's world accessible to the viewer/reader. Here is a 12-year-old girl talking about the disc:

HANNAH	The music tells you it is about horror . . . and tells you the period it was from – it was sort of medievalish.

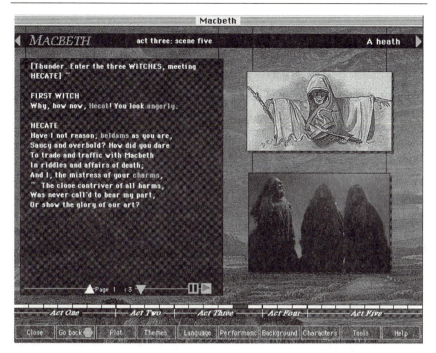

Figure 5.2 Wiches on the heath: text and moving image in a scene from *Macbeth*

INTERVIEWER   What about the backdrop?

HANNAH   It is depressing scenery, bleak like a wasteland, it reminds me of the moors, quite scary, like you're on the moors in the middle of a storm.

INTERVIEWER   What do you learn from the video clip?

HANNAH   You can see they are bad, they are in a storm, the voice tells you she's quite old, she's not posh – she's an outcast – left to live in a cave or something – her voice is gravelly and rough – she might be ill or something ... without the pictures you would not really know what they looked like, they could be young and beautiful, they could be like Medusa or a talking frog – you can tell who's speaking and things like who has got a limp ... when you are reading you might say it really fast ... you might say it the wrong way, put the full stops in the wrong places.

Of course this response creates a problem – is it not the job of the reader to create the pictures that go with the text? This is one that the designers seem to be aware of. Clips from different versions of the play are provided, including a Zulu production on another section of the disc, but these too are someone else's representations. It is an issue which children are also aware of – perhaps children have more understanding of image and imagery than we give them credit for:

> There's not a certain way to see the play . . . what you see on disc is not necessarily what they look like. They are fictional characters, it's up to you, there isn't a right way they should be like. You might imagine them different from the video . . . what you see is the idea of the person who did the performance, not what they really are.

> (Hannah)

In the *Macbeth* disc, we liked the way in which text, music and image combined to give a coherent picture of the play – our only proviso being that the existing storage capacity of CD-ROM means that there is a restriction on the amount of video which could be used. With more storage capacity will the moving images have even greater importance? This is something suggested by Dale Spender (1995). However, the printed text seemed to us important as it enabled users to go back and look at individual words or sentences more easily. More importantly, the printed text served as the reference point for the interpretation of the staged production, for example, what was there in the text which supported the idea that the witches are bad or are outcasts? Can alternative interpretations of the witches be considered?

The World of Number

Stories and story telling within CD-ROM are not confined to the world of literature. In *Discovering India*, for example, students could identify with the story of Sampangi as they follow his move away from a rural village to Bangalore. Meanwhile, the power of story telling was neatly illustrated for us in the history disc *Stowaway*. This disc contains many sound effects, animations and hot spots. However, the child we saw using the disc was engrossed in the Captain's diary – a simple linear story in printed text of life at sea. The story telling idea resurfaces within several other discs; one idea which seemed largely underused was that of story telling by peers, but this did come up in the *World of Number* discs.

The World of Number is a set of four CD titles designed at the Shell Centre, University of Nottingham (the materials were originally produced in interactive video format – see Chapter 2). In one disc, *Number Puzzles*, students are introduced to several mathematical investigations through a short video clip. The clip shows a group of young people trying an investigation which the viewer is then expected to try. When working with this disc (for an extended discussion, see Hammond 1995b) we found that students identified with the personalities on screen and were drawn into the 'story'. The majority of students' comments were favourable:

I think of adults as being clever and it puts me off. If I see that children can do it we might be able to do it, too.

(Year 10 girl)

It is more interesting . . . it makes you want to have a go yourself.

(Year 10 girl)

All the students who used it with us thought the games had been scripted and that the children they saw were trying to remember their lines. However, they did not find the talk too stilted and most realised there would be a lack of clarity if more than one person spoke at the same time as would happen in a more natural setting. (This was an important consideration as the quality of the video clips was poor on the machines being used.) Two of the older students felt that the presentation did not work; it was a good idea but did not come over. One of these was critical of the way that adults used young people to give credibility to something they had designed.

Olson (1988) draws the distinction between *expressive* teaching acts, which convey messages about how teachers wish to be seen by their students, and *instrumental* teaching acts, which are directed at learning. The video clips were expressive in their use of young people to present the problem. The instrumental role of the film was to introduce the rules of the game and to illustrate that it should be played with physical objects. The concept of the game was not difficult but the demonstration was appreciated by all the groups, all of whom were Year 10 pupils.

It's clearer with people . . . better than paper. It's different – you take it in more.

You know what you are expected to achieve. It's easier to understand than reading.

It's better to have the picture; it makes it clearer. Writing doesn't always explain it.

It gives you a more physical understanding of the problem. On paper you don't feel as if you have much to do with it at all.

The clips we saw were not always clear, the discussion on the clips was stilted and only a very limited amount of footage could be used. Despite these limitations the *Number Puzzles* were successful in drawing students into the activity and point to the potential of developing new types of instructional materials which are more discursive and make use of peer tutoring.

Access to processes, concepts and experiments

Here we continue our theme of access by looking at some examples of science discs. The use of multimedia in science teaching and learning can extend access to learners in at least three ways: by letting them see processes which may be too fast, too slow or too dangerous to observe 'live', in real time; by helping to explain and illustrate some of the difficult concepts in science; and by allowing them to 'do' experiments that would otherwise be impossible.

Our examples show how access is extended but they also raise three more contentious issues: the replacement of traditional practical 'scientific' activity by the use of multimedia to create virtual laboratories; the consequent danger of misrepresentation of science and scientific activity; and the potential of multimedia images of scientific concepts not only to help learners but also to create misconceptions.

Out of the lab and into the multimedia system?

A number of CD-ROMs for science now allow quite detailed 'virtual experiments' to be done successfully and repeatedly on screen, without using up any of the consumables which science teachers can ill afford to buy. This can be an attraction to some pupils, particularly those who detest traditional practical work:

> I like being able to do things over and over again, without anybody being able to see me . . . and it always works.
>
> (Year 10 pupil)

The key issues are whether this devalues scientific activity by removing some of the real, hands-on, authentic business of science and placing it in the realm of multimedia, and whether the images of scientific method and process portrayed in this way are a distortion of the reality of science.

For example, the *Motion* disc and *Forces and Effects* contain experiments that are either impossible or unsafe for school labs and hence (in the view of some teachers) they more than earn their money. Similarly, *The Chemistry Set* contains several 'surrogate experiments' and demonstrations such as dropping caesium into water (see Figure 5.3) and combining hydrogen with fluorine – both of which are dramatic but dangerous to perform in the laboratory. How can this help pupils?

> It would help you writing up experiments . . . instead of just being told the order [of reactivity of metals]. You can see it for yourself so it stays in your head better.
>
> (Year 10 pupil)

> with the CD-ROM you get to see the good ones when the glass breaks [caesium in water] and good sound effects, you can hear them clearer. You can't do a replay in the lab . . . here you can slow it down step by step and catch everything.
>
> (Year 10 pupil)

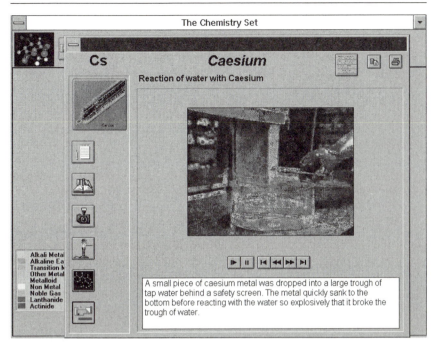

The Chemistry Set

Cs   *Caesium*
Reaction of water with Caesium

Alkali Metal
Alkaline Ea
Transition M
Other Metal
Metalloid
Non Metal
Noble Gas
Lanthanide
Actinide

A small piece of caesium metal was dropped into a large trough of tap water behind a safety screen. The metal quickly sank to the bottom before reacting with the water so explosively that it broke the trough of water.

Figure 5.3 A still from a *Chemistry Set* video clip (with sound) of caesium being dropped into water – a 'virtual demonstration'

Even experiments which can be done for real in the lab are, in the view of one pupil at least, better done on the screen:

> You get to see it as it should be . . . my teacher sometimes says: 'That wasn't meant to happen'. So he *tells* you what should happen. With the CD-ROM you're guaranteed to see what ought to happen.
>
> (Year 10 pupil)

One chemistry teacher appreciated the value of multimedia clips of dangerous events for safety, but lamented the loss of smell:

> I can't do things like this in the lab any more, especially using things that smell, with so many asthmatic pupils and so forth. Using multimedia demos means that [the pupils] can see it as many times as they like. But they still do miss out on the sense of smell. Some don't even know what ammonia smells like.

Motion focuses on more than fifty video sequences of moving objects which involve forces: cars colliding; golf, tennis and footballs being struck; spinning objects; gymnasts and weight lifters; rockets and astronauts. These all present attractive, sporty images (incidentally, with a male soccer player and female tennis player: Figure 5.4). The moving sequences can be studied again and again just for the sheer enjoyment of seeing the stresses and strains involved. Each sequence can be studied in slow motion, backwards or forwards, all at once or frame by frame. Younger students enjoy clips in *Motions and Effects* such as the falling chimney (Figure 5.5), or the ball being compressed just as it is struck. The disc is valuable just to introduce them to forces and their effects:

> It's not really practical to do it [experiments with moving objects] in school . . . you can't slow it down. You wouldn't be able to see it [the football] properly being squashed and you wouldn't be able to measure the velocity of the ball. It shows you things you couldn't see with just the eye.
>
> (Year 10 pupil)

The disc's unique feature is its analysis software which allows older pupils to study the movement quantitatively. On each moving image points can be marked using the mouse. Positions and their times can be tabulated and then processed, either to display a graph or to provide the data for calculations (Figure 5.6). Thus velocities, accelerations, forces, kinetic energy, and momentum can be worked out for cars, trains, balls, rockets; indeed, if it moves it can be worked on.

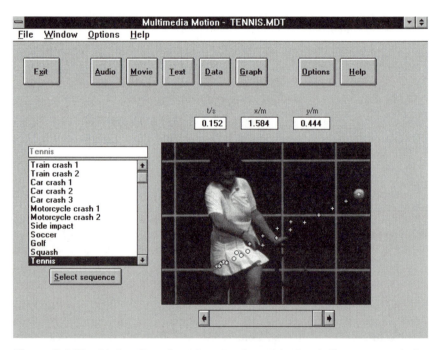

Figure 5.4 The *Motion* disc allows learners to watch closely the movement of a tennis ball and (if required) to analyse it quantitatively

You can put arrows on it and work out speeds and acceleration and stuff. You can't do things like that on a video – you've just got to watch it happen.
(Year 10 pupil)

This is the innovative aspect of a disc of this nature, which helps to move CD-ROM use in science forward from the passive entertainment mode to interactivity and truly provides 'added-value' over traditional school practical work. One teacher commented:

It's far easier, and safer, to do this on screen and take measurements, than doing it in a lab. It also plots graphs which can take some pupils an age to do . . . and it's easier for class control than running trolleys down wooden ramps.

Forces and Effects also contains scope for plenty of interactivity with its *Virtual Laboratory* of more than eighteen experiments. Some are potentially dangerous and so are best done from the safety of a mouse and keyboard. Others could be done in the lab but the value of having them on disc is that they can be tried and repeated over and over again, changing the variables involved indefinitely.

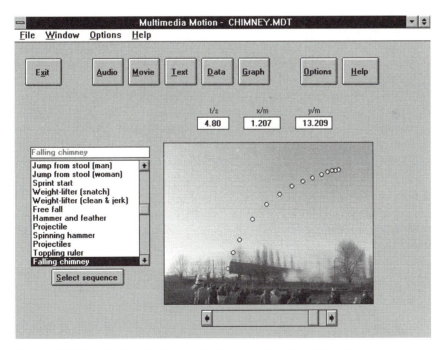

Figure 5.5 The *Motion* disc is genuinely interactive: by clicking the mouse, markers can be placed on different points of the chimney at regular time intervals to analyse in detail the way it falls

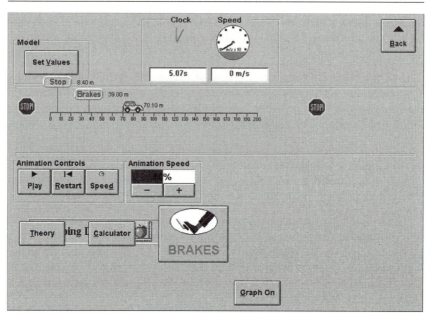

Figure 5.6 The *Forces and Effects* disc allows users to do 'virtual experiments' over and over again

> You can change things quicker and easier . . . it's more accurate doing it on the screen.
>
> (Year 10 pupil)

> It's easier . . . and you can do a wider range of stuff, like changing the mass of the car and its speed, or its brakes and things; and you don't have to draw your own graph . . . it's instant and they're more accurate; the graphs show things clearly.
>
> (Year 10 pupil)

However, some teachers remarked that fairly simple, traditional experiments, such as measuring the extension of a spring with weights on it, should be done 'for real':

> If my pupils used multimedia all the time they would never learn to use their hands and to do simple manipulative jobs like screwing a clamp to a stand or taking the top out of an acid bottle.

One pupil was clear about what should be done 'live' and what should be 'virtual':

> With a CD-ROM, it's not like doing the experiment yourself, it's not live. If you can do them yourself, I think you should; but if a teacher

has to do it, or you're just told about it, it ought to be on here [CD-ROM].

If relied on exclusively, the use of such CD-ROMs in science teaching would displace important labour, i.e. hands-on experimenting, investigating and the opportunity to develop manipulative skills. But if multimedia use is a *complement* to good practical work rather than a replacement for it, then its place in science can be justified and it will add value, not take it away.

More generally though, to what extent will the use of discs for this kind of 'virtual practical work' affect pupils' views of science and scientific activity? Do they present it as 'clean and unproblematic' when in reality it is a messy, highly problematic venture?

Messages about science

The old adage of school science practicals – 'If it moves it's Biology, if it smells it's Chemistry, if it doesn't work it's Physics' – becomes obsolete with multimedia. Living things do not inhabit CD-ROMs, smell is not yet an output of computer systems, and the virtual physics experiments of discs such as *Forces and Effects* and *Motion* never go wrong. Thus we have animals (and human beings in many programs) which can be dissected and taken apart at will without offending any ethical codes. We have all the chemical reactions whose smells seem to stick forever in our memories of school life (remember sulphur dioxide and hydrogen sulphide?) re-created but in sound and vision only; and we have the experiments of physics such as stretching springs, measuring speeds and connecting electric circuits working every time and repeatable at will. Students will need to find new jokes and insults to aim at the science teacher in the white coat (which, incidentally, becomes unnecessary).

This is obviously an overstatement of the practical shifts that could result from multimedia use in science. But analyses of media coverage (especially in the newspapers) of science show that it is portrayed as 'whizz-bang and dramatic; a disconnected rag-bag of work and discovery; certain; individual; and sudden, not based on earlier work' (Wellington 1991: 370; these points are expanded in that article). There is a danger that growing multimedia use in education will add to that portrayal. In reality scientific experiments are extremely difficult to repeat and replicate successfully and they do often go wrong; science usually proceeds slowly and carefully, by accretion; it is largely based on teamwork rather than individual 'crackpot' discoveries; and it is often a very messy, inexact and unclean activity.

One of the stated requirements of the England and Wales National Curriculum is to teach pupils about the nature of science and scientific ideas. Exclusive use of multimedia to replace hands-on practical activity will produce a distorted view of the nature of science and fail to fulfil this statutory requirement.

The power of images to create misconceptions

Images have the power to mislead as well as to motivate or educate. Some of the more difficult and abstract concepts of science are increasingly being portrayed on screen by multimedia applications. The portrayal may involve an attractive and attention-grabbing animation. But can these images, often of abstract concepts, breed misconceptions? For example, in *Electricity and Magnetism* electric current is shown in blue and red. The red current comes from the positive side of a battery, then becomes blue after 'travelling through' a bulb or other device (Figure 5.7). Current is thus depicted as a steady stream of particles shown by dots on the screen leaving a battery, changing colour and then returning back to the other pole of the battery (negative). Animations and analogies can be valuable in teaching difficult concepts. But the danger is that learners will see this as the 'correct representation' of electric current rather than an analogy to help understanding. One pupil asked: 'Does current change from red to blue after it goes through a light bulb?'

A teacher was concerned that the current animation could be reversed, by 'playing it' backwards: 'My pupils will think that current from a battery can travel both ways, and we can change its direction.' She said that she would not use this program for that reason.

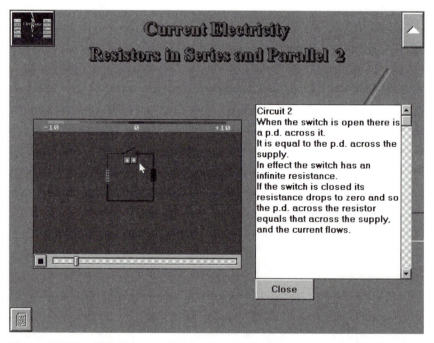

Figure 5.7 The *Electricity and Magnetism* disc enables the abstract concept of electric current to be visualised, animated and 'played with' on the screen

Access to other people, cultures and experiences

Pris sur le vif

Pris sur le vif is a package designed to promote language skills and motivate pupils in French in the first two years of learning the language.

The first impression from viewing the disc is the sense of a textbook coming alive, with each section working as an integral part of the whole. Instead of listening to voices and perhaps looking at photographs, or using our imagination to conjure up a body to go with the voice, the person is there, alive and speaking to us directly. The quotes included here are from Year 10 pupils talking about the disc.

> The voices sound more human than those on tapes and there's a picture to help you understand what the word's about.

> It's an alternative to boring work. It's not plain, cos of pictures – people talking makes it more interesting than working through books.

> The picture helps you remember the word.

Less effort is required in linguistic terms but the cultural images are more powerful. The overall image conveyed in the application is the sense of France and French-speaking Canada as part of a global community, with hints of a cultural context which is unique and one that deserves respect and celebration. The emphasis is on the human with close-up moving pictures of young people in the main talking about their lives.

> It's good to see how the accents are different – Paris and Quebec French – and how fast the speed . . . how fast the people speak.

The sense of location is portrayed by the background to the close-ups of individuals. The Eiffel Tower appears several times as an icon conveying a sense of glamour and the notion of a power centre (in one instance as the backdrop to a recording studio). Cultural images are assimilated subliminally and in the video clips the language washes over the user. This is acceptable though, as all language learning has a cultural as well as linguistic objective and the linguistic takes front stage once the initial messages have been presented and we get onto the language tasks.

The emphasis is clearly on youth and school and leisure pursuits moving in each case from the general to the particular, the social to the individual (Figure 5.8).

> There are so many different topics on it . . . there's music and young people.

The process of distillation is in favour of the presentation of a positive cultural image with no emphasis on social problems or ordinary working life; however,

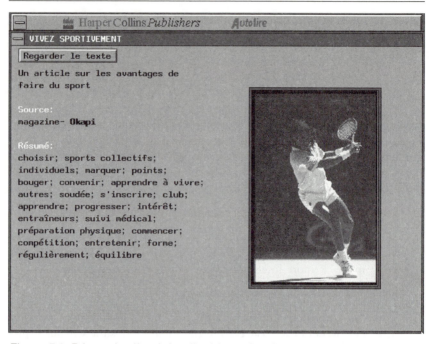

Figure 5.8 Pris sur le vif and *Autolire* (shown here) present positive images of young people in other countries and cultures

this reflects the spirit of early language learning which often makes advanced study of issues more difficult. Many of the areas covered can be linked to the most popular images conveyed in advertising: 'Happy families, rich luxurious lifestyles, dreams and fantasy, successful romance and love, glamorous places, success in career or job, art culture and history, nature and the natural world, beautiful women' (Dyer 1982). The last area quoted is a notable exception in that we are presented with non-stereotypical images of young women and other races. A good gender and racial balance pervades the application with young women and young black people having an equal voice in status-giving contexts. There are shots of girls speaking in the foreground with computers acting as a backdrop. There is a photograph of two black students studying in a library. In a physics lesson there is a black girl sitting at the front studying circuits.

The sense of difference comes across in positive ways: the French kiss ('la bise'), French food, the use of Minitel in the home, architecture in the street and in the home. There is a lovely shot of a young person riding up to her apartment in a large residential building in an old lift.

The video clips and stills help to promote the culture in a more positive way than, say, viewing a video tape in class, because the students can move around and explore them in a non-linear way; the learners have control and can go back and interact with interesting aspects as many times as they wish. Each linguistic task is given added cultural dimension because the task is presented by a different native speaker each time. While the experience will not feel the same as being in the country where the visitor is the distiller of information, the image is designed to motivate and incite cultural curiosity, a goal that is realised in this application because of the unique features of multimedia. A pupil here talks of getting 'into' the language:

> It's easier to use than just copying out all the language from the black-board and it helps you. It gives you exercises that are easy to do and everything . . . like you get into all of the language.

DISCUSSION AND CONCLUSIONS

We have looked at two main areas: the way that the images, sounds and words used in multimedia can support learning and extend access in several ways, and the power of images to represent or misrepresent. We have argued, using specific examples, that the 'new' features of multimedia can have great value in enhancing learning and motivation, although it is not always easy to specify and articulate their value. We have used verbatim quotes from pupils and teachers to try to illustrate the connection between image and learning. However, we have also cited examples of multimedia applications using images or animations which may have unwanted, undesirable impacts on learning – either by creating misconceptions or by falsely portraying or representing a concept or a culture.

Our view is that multimedia can be a powerful 'tool' in learning if used carefully and with appropriate intervention and caution. This is the theme of the next section.

Developing a 'critical media literacy' in pupils and students

One of the main points to emerge in this chapter is our suggestion that children should develop a critical awareness and understanding of what they are seeing, hearing and reading when they use multimedia in terms of *where it came from, how it got there,* and *who put it there.* (A detailed framework on these lines for analysing any curriculum material is put forward by Winter (1997), based on McDowell (1994).) This awareness, for teachers and pupils, is part of a 'critical media literacy' which McLaren (1995: 22) argues should 'provide students with the symbolic resources for creative and social forma-tion in order that they can more critically re-enter the vast, uncharted spaces of common culture'.

This idea is illustrated in a practical context by Jeannette Ayton (1996) in an interesting report of work in a UK primary school. She argues that 'children should learn about the media because their understanding of the world is largely shaped by the media's audio-visual messages. Our language-based curriculum is no longer adequate . . . we need to devise a new parity between visual and verbal literacies' (Ayton 1996: 21). How can we do this?

Multi-modality and multimedia: messages from pictures, messages from words

An illustration of how pictures and words can convey different messages is shown in this example:

> At the crisis point during negotiations to settle an important industrial dispute, a representative of the employers was called straight from a banquet to a televised confrontation with union leaders. His dinner jacket and bow tie clashed strongly with his words, which stressed that the industry had no money to increase the pay of workers. However forceful his arguments, the visual image left with the viewers was affluent: the two minutes it would have taken to change his jacket, shirt and tie would have paid off in greater public attention to his ideas.
>
> (Morgan and Welton 1986: 14)

If pupils are to become reflective and critical users of multimedia they need to be encouraged to look at what information is given in each mode. Do the pictures tell one 'story', and the words another? To examine this in the classroom, teachers might arrange for learners to watch the pictures without the sound, to see what information they pick up, and then listen to the sound without seeing the pictures. Another suggestion is to get (where possible) the pupils themselves to change the music, the sound or the background – and record their new impressions of the whole text.

As well as *what* is conveyed in each channel, there is the question of *how* it is conveyed. Kress and van Leeuwen (1996) point out that visual and verbal communication cannot both do exactly the same things:

> The meanings which can be realised in language and in visual communication overlap in part, that is, some things can be expressed both visually and verbally; and in part they diverge – some things can be 'said' only visually, others only verbally. But even when something can be 'said' both visually and verbally the *way in which* it will be said is different.
>
> (Kress and van Leeuwen 1996: 2, original emphasis)

Visual and verbal literacy

Past lessons from multimedia (and textbook) use indicate that children remember more, are more active, and enjoy more, when they experience both pictures and words together (see Chapter 2). In 1964, McLuhan said:

> Today it is inconceivable that any publication, daily or periodical, could hold more than a few thousand readers without pictures. . . . Would it

not seem natural and necessary that the young be provided with at least as much training of perception in this graphic and photographic world as they get in the typographic? In fact, they need more training in graphics, because the art of casting and arranging actors in ads is both complex and forcefully insidious. . . . Highly literate people cannot cope with the non-verbal art of the pictorial, so they dance impatiently up and down to express a pointless disapproval that renders them futile and gives new power and authority to the ads. . . . The fact that typography is itself mainly subliminal in effect and that pictures are, as well, is a secret that is safe from the book-oriented community.

(McLuhan 1964: 230–1)

But semiotics and visual analysis has moved on from this view. Many theorists now see pictures and graphics as literacies which we largely lack the vocabulary to talk about. Our view is that we rarely give pupils the opportunity to talk about what they see – but it comes out quite articulately when they are given the chance. We do not seem to be moving from verbal literacy to a purely visual literacy, but towards a world of multimodality – a world of complex texts where pictures increasingly interact with words, where pictures and words work together and reinterpret each other (Goodman 1996). So increased visual literacy *is* important, but not because the verbal is becoming obsolete. Guy Cook (discussing McLuhan) says: 'Not only have pictures gained ground, but also language, where it is used, leans further and further towards the meanings it derives from interaction with pictures' (Cook 1992: 49). As an example, he discusses the widespread use of visual puns in advertising in this respect – the pictures rely on their interaction with the verbal text for their impact.

Text-based literacy is achieved only through intensive education and training, at school and at home. In contrast, competence in *visual* literacy in the classroom, and in society, is more or less ignored. The cause is partly political, connected with ideas or ideologies about what is 'valuable' for education. Formal education has stressed that which can be standardised and measured. Images, and our reactions to them, are difficult to standardise and measure, so education and the curriculum marginalise them:

> The skill of producing [visual] texts of this kind, however important their role in contemporary society, is not taught in schools. In terms of this new visual literacy, education produces illiterates.
>
> (Kress and van Leeuwen 1996: 1)

Kress and van Leeuwen (1996) have outlined how we *can* talk about images (still and moving images) in terms of a grammar, or sentences, consisting of subjects, verbs and objects – in other words, as stories. In addition, students who have followed media studies courses will have developed some of the vocabulary and the language of 'framing', 'cropping', 'juxtaposition' and so on. Our belief is that, given the opportunity, children really can 'talk a good picture'.

Questions when considering image and portrayal on CD-ROM

As a summary to the previous two sections we offer a set of questions to be raised in critically examining multimedia applications:

- What messages do images convey, e.g. about a country; about a discipline such as science; about a 'race', if there is such a thing?
- How much care has been taken in the choice and selection of the images on screen? Why, i.e. on what grounds, were the images selected?
- Do multimedia authors choose images less carefully than words? Do learners view images less carefully than words?
- How are images framed? What has been excluded or cut off, e.g. pylons from a beautiful view.
- What purpose does an image or animation serve? What added-value do sounds and images provide? On the other hand, what misconceptions might an image create?
- Do images replace text or supplement and complement it?
- Does the use of multimedia displace important, 'authentic' activity, e.g. first-hand experience, for learners?

CAPTURING, PRESENTING AND 'COMMODIFYING KNOWLEDGE': THE IMPACT OF TECHNOLOGY ON WHAT COUNTS AS KNOWLEDGE AND HOW IT IS PACKAGED

Advances in knowledge, often scientific knowledge, have clearly led to progression and advancement in technology. The history of technology in two areas illustrates this clearly: transport, most notably cars and aeroplanes; and IT, most notably through the development of processing technology (chips) and communications technology (fibre optics, microwaves and so on). But little thought has been given to the way in which technology in a sense retaliates and influences, often determines, the future construction of knowledge.

First, technology determines *what* knowledge is acquired. Thus the making of the telescope, the development of the rocket and the invention of the electron microscope have all shaped, and will continue to shape, the knowledge which humans construct and the territory in which they can construct it. Rocket technology, for example, has extended the domain in which humans can construct knowledge to include most of the solar system. Similarly, technology determines *how* knowledge is acquired and to some extent how much; technology also determines how, and how much, knowledge can be processed. For example, data-collection techniques in science and medicine can probe parts and probe phenomena that earlier instruments have been unable to reach – for example, phenomena which take place incredibly quickly or which occur in extremely hostile environments. New data-collection technology can also greatly accelerate the rate at which information is collected. This allows vastly increased amounts of data to be collected, e.g. on the atmosphere, a human, a chemical process, which in turn has led to the demand for greater processing power – a demand met by the advancement of technology for data processing, i.e. the chip. A classic example here is our knowledge of the world's weather – still the butt of many a joke, but none the less vastly more reliable than it was in the mid-1980s.

The crucial point for this book is that multimedia technology will not only represent and portray knowledge now and in the future, but also shape it and determine it. As multimedia proliferates, that which can be digitised and computerised will be that which is packaged, presented, taught and learnt – at home or at school.

Usher and Edwards (1994) present this as one of the features of education in a post-modern age:

> The proliferation of computers with their own logic and prescriptions actually impacts upon what can legitimately be called knowledge because knowledge has to be in a form which can be computerised.
>
> (Usher and Edwards 1994: 174)

This in turn affects the relationship between individual learners and knowledge:

> The relationship of the suppliers and users of knowledge to the knowledge they supply and use is now tending, and will increasingly tend, to assume the form already taken by the relationship of commodity producers and consumers to the commodities they produce and consume.
>
> (Lyotard, quoted in Usher and Edwards 1994: 174)

Just as the supermarket chains shape the commodities we buy and the way we eat, will the spread of multimedia determine the knowledge which is presented to us and the way we 'consume' it? The medium would then actually determine the message.

But this is too pessimistic a note on which to end. As Goodman (1996: 38) rightly points out: 'Technological advances have brought in their wake . . . a vast increase in the use of visual information for communicative purposes.'

There is in fact no evidence of a decline in sales of books (other than school textbooks) and magazines. One medium adds to another and extends the range of resources available in schools and in homes. Goodman discusses (1996: 38–105) constructive ways in which visual and verbal literacies interact and can be developed side by side. The challenge for education is that people should learn, at least partly in the formal curriculum, to examine all the sources they use (books, magazines and multimedia) in a critical way – perhaps bearing in mind some of the frameworks we have suggested above.

Part III

Teachers, multimedia and schools

Chapter 6

Teachers and multimedia

A consistent picture which emerges from earlier chapters of the book is the role of the teacher in exploiting multimedia effectively in the classroom. Past work on professional development and IT (e.g. Bliss *et al.* 1986; Ellam and Wellington 1986; Scaife and Wellington 1993) has highlighted the difficulties that teachers have in introducing IT into their teaching. This work has illustrated the importance of understanding the teacher perspective on both technology and change.

This chapter will explore how teachers have reacted to multimedia in the classroom and the difficulties they have experienced. In particular we look at teachers' expertise and enthusiasm for using multimedia and report on their experiences of getting started with CD-ROMs. We go on to look at teachers' views on introducing multimedia to learners and their reflections, including worries about curriculum fit, on the software which is currently available. Finally we look at the emerging impact of multimedia in the home on the teacher's role in the classroom.

LEVELS OF EXPERIENCE, ENTHUSIASM AND COMPETENCE AMONG TEACHERS

Teacher types

Many past publications on IT in education have stressed the importance of the context in which teachers operate. Olson (1988: 13) for example writes: 'We need to know about the "school worlds" in which teachers work. Only then can we properly appraise the potential on microcomputers. We need to know more about how the computer and classroom cultures interact.'

With this in mind, Olson and others have offered various typologies, in some cases caricatures, of varying teacher attitudes towards IT. Bliss *et al.* (1986), for example, examined the factors which influenced the introduction of computers into one school in the early 1980s. They classified seven different types of teachers: 'the favourable, the critical, the worried, the unfavourable, the antagonistic, the indifferent, and the uninitiated'. They went on to paint two fictional portraits of Mr Joule and Mr Mikado (note the pseudonyms and gender) who are at opposite ends of the spectrum in their views on computer use in education (Bliss *et al.* 1986: 52). Similar fictitious categorisations, with suitable pseudonyms, have been put forward in the past by Wellington (1985: 16) and Olson (1988).

Responses to multimedia

Little has changed. As the following two factual cameos demonstrate, teachers' attitudes to multimedia technology may range from total enthusiasm and commitment to equally passionate rejection of anything related to IT.

The enthusiastic IT user

Rachel represents the epitome of the IT enthusiast. Now in her late twenties Rachel belongs to a generation who grew up with computers. Introduced to computing while in primary school, technology is an integral part of her life both at home and work. Rachel has a home page on the Web and is building up a network of links with colleagues around the world. Her latest acquisition is an electronic notebook with which she attempts to organise her new responsibilities as IT co-ordinator in a large inner city school. In devising the IT policy, Rachel is anxious to ensure that the school develops and maintains a position at the cutting edge of the technology. She argues vociferously for extra resources and finds it difficult to understand why others are less than totally committed to using technology as an integral aspect of their teaching. When asked to comment about the use of multimedia in schools Rachel's enthusiasm and commitment are clear. 'Multimedia CD-ROMs are an extremely exciting way to learn and they allow children access to information that would otherwise not be possible.' However, she is frustrated at the pace of change which is taking place in schools. 'There should be a machine in every classroom. Schools should be taking the lead in information technology and not lagging behind the home market.' She looks forward to a time when every child will have access to the Internet at school and logging on will be a daily event.

The antagonistic IT user

At the other end of the continuum Betty is antagonistic to anything related to IT. In school her colleagues assume that Betty is afraid of the technology; however, while she is nervous of any unfamiliar machinery, the underlying problem is that she does not understand the role of the new technology. Technology; has no place in her teaching, her life or her thinking. She tried to work with the BBC computer that was introduced to her school in the early 1980s but the technology was not user friendly and the early training courses served only to increase her feelings of inadequacy. Now she prefers to leave the technology to other younger staff with the consequence that Betty often feels excluded from staffroom conversations. She does not have access to the discourse of computers. Moreover, she knows that her colleagues will not understand her view that computers are little more than expensive 'toys for the boys'.

Rachel's and Betty's attitudes represent positions at either end of a continuum. The following quotes from secondary school teachers illustrate the kinds of teachers who lie along this continuum:

> I have used multimedia software at times but find I am still worried about how to organise the class into groups to work on the machine.

> I like the idea of multimedia but found reasons for not using it. It's a 'lovely idea' but . . .

And perhaps even more cautious:

> I've rejected the idea. It's fine for others but I can't afford the time for such luxuries.

> I've tried it, but I'm worried about losing control over the students. They were all over the place when they got back to the normal routine of lessons. It took me ages to pull it back together.

However, a survey commissioned by NCET (1996) suggests that the majority of teachers are neither committed enthusiasts nor dyed in the wool sceptics. Instead they appear to hold a position somewhere in the middle of the continuum, a position or series of positions which we call 'cautious enthusiasm'. In the context of this chapter 'cautious enthusiasm' will be used to signify those teachers who welcome multimedia technology and want to find ways of integrating it into their teaching but, for one reason or another, have some reservations about the technology itself, its usefulness in teaching and learning, or the level of support which is provided to the teachers and pupils who work with technology.

Understanding and finding ways to address these concerns is central to furthering the development of multimedia technology in schools. Consequently, the remainder of this chapter examines issues raised by cautious enthusiasts under various headings.

TEACHER REFLECTIONS ON GETTING STARTED WITH CD-ROM

Go for it!

Some cautious enthusiasts have been pleasantly surprised at the ease with which they have been able to introduce multimedia technology into their own classrooms:

Planning work for the class has not been as difficult as I feared. To start with, most children learn a lot by finding their own way around the material. Headphones have to be used, though – otherwise the class are continually distracted.

(Cheshire teacher)

Teachers we interviewed often offered helpful advice for other teachers who were considering introducing CD-ROM into their schools. The message was predominantly one of enthusiastic encouragement: teachers should 'go for it' because CD-ROM has 'enormous potential' and is 'a wonderful asset'; 'children really like it' and 'its use is only limited by the imagination'. However, many respondents stressed that teachers should make a point of previewing particular software before purchasing, as they had found the quality and relevance to be very variable. Teachers should always work through any program themselves before introducing it to children. If possible, teachers should visit schools where a CD-ROM system is already in use, to see and hear how it is being employed and to preview software. As well as providing a useful basis for children's activities, the content of CD-ROM software could be a valuable resource for teachers themselves when preparing lessons or materials.

Learn by doing

All the teachers we interviewed stressed the importance of 'hands-on training' for teachers. Having the opportunity to 'play' with the technology at home during a holiday was also thought to be beneficial. However, it has to be recognised that this approach would not suit teachers who are reluctant to use the technology.

I got into a lot of trouble with my wife, but I really enjoyed it and I was enthusiastic but it is difficult to get other people to, I mean I have said 'If you have got it next term take it home in the holidays. You can't break it'. But people say 'Oh I don't know, what if I can't do this or if I can't do that? There is nobody there to help me'.

(Sheffield teacher)

Many teachers have found that they can learn a lot from watching children. It is often easier to learn from children at home than in school.

A colleague of ours has said exactly the same. He has taken the CD-ROM home during the holiday and he has got a 9-year-old son who is computer literate and he says 'I have learnt more from my son than I have learnt by doing it myself'. Because his son is not frightened to click it there and everywhere and have a look to see what happens when you do this.

(Sheffield teacher)

This kind of fearless exploration is invaluable in learning to use the technology. The difficulty for advisers and in-service training (INSET) providers is to attempt to create the conditions in which reluctant teachers are prepared to 'have a go'. One solution might be in providing teachers with their own laptop computers (for example, the NCET has piloted the Multimedia Portables for School scheme), though this must seem a remote possibility for many teachers.

Many teachers see hands-on experiential learning as a major turning point in accepting and using multimedia technology.

> Most of my knowledge of CD-ROM systems comes from owning my own. I spend hours at home 'playing' with software on floppy and CD. Without this I could not have used the CD-ROM systems as fully as I do. Where this 'homework' is not possible I would imagine school machines would be under used – there is no time in primary education for experimenting.
>
> (Leicestershire primary teacher)

Advice to less enthusiastic colleagues is invariably to 'go and see the benefits of the technology for yourself'.

> Go and 'play' on one at another school. Talk to the staff, but watch the pupils. Their enthusiasm will be infectious. Their learning in terms of skills and National Curriculum contents will impress you enormously.
>
> (Leicestershire teacher)

Unfortunately, the endless cycle of teaching, marking and preparation leaves teachers little time to explore the technology in school. While enthusiastic teachers will welcome the opportunity to take the school computer home in the holiday, cautious enthusiasts may find this threatening, especially if it means working without technical support if things go wrong. Without personal hands-on experience teachers are forced to fall back on the expertise of the children in their class with computers at home. The obvious, but relatively expensive, answer is to provide teachers with in-service training.

The need for in-service support

Teachers are aware of the need for INSET to provide time for them to evaluate available discs and perhaps see them in action; teachers would like INSET providers to have some expertise and focus on their particular subject or the age group they teach.

> We felt that more specific training in perhaps one, or at the most two, discs would be better with time for individual 'hands-on' experience. We need to discuss the suitability of the discs chosen by someone with an overall recognition of primary school matters.
>
> (Bolton primary teacher)

An awareness of available discs is essential but not sufficient. Teachers also need opportunities to reflect on the potential of multimedia technology.

> As with most things, you need to be fully aware of the possibilities inherent in the CD-ROM. Using one is fairly simple but the potential is enormous. You need to know the discs you intend using and be prepared to support colleagues in making them aware of the possibilities.

> Training is needed for everyone in both basic computer skills (technical) and in the *purposes* of using a CD-ROM. Otherwise they can become pretty, but expensive, occupiers of children.
>
> (Bolton IT co-ordinator)

In addition to INSET, teachers would welcome ongoing in-school support in the form of computer-trained teachers in every school and user friendly manuals.

> We received a huge box full of manuals covering all sorts of things we are unlikely to use. However, the very thin multimedia manual was not as detailed as it could be. It did not explain accurately how to add a new CD to the system.
>
> (Wirral IT co-ordinator)

There is also a need for technical support in the form of a helpline or a paid technician, which some schools (especially in the secondary sector) are fortunate enough to have. The alternative may be the 'unpaid technician', i.e. the pupil.

TEACHERS SUPPORTING STUDENTS' DEVELOPMENT AND ACCESS

One of the major issues for all teachers is the extent to which they can support pupil development with and through multimedia software. 'Cautious experts' in particular wonder what role they have to play in supporting learners who may well have more experience and/or fewer inhibitions related to using the technology. 'Cautious enthusiasts' are often only too aware of how confident and competent learners of all ages can be with the technology. As a teacher in Oxfordshire points out, 'Most teachers are not computer experts; very often the children are more competent'. Moreover, most teachers are aware that they have much to learn from their pupils. Recognising this fact is a challenge to many teachers, especially in an area where they feel less than totally competent. However, there are limitations in the expertise of children.

Anxiety about their relative lack of skills might lead teachers to overestimate children's competencies. Not all children are computer literate or confident. While some may spend a lot of their free time logged on to their computers at home, a number do not. Moreover, there are a minority of children who seem reluctant to engage with the technology, preferring to sit as passive observers in small group activities. Teachers need to be aware of the range of competencies in their classrooms and to devise strategies which draw on the strengths of the 'expert' while simultaneously empowering the less able. A typical strategy in many classrooms is to use the more knowledgeable pupil to teach other children in the group how to navigate a disc. This will work well as long as the pupil-tutor understands the role as helping another child become a user of the machine and not a passive observer. The teacher has a role in monitoring the group to try to ensure this is happening.

There is a danger of reading too much into pupil expertise. Just because children are computer literate does not mean that they will understand the aims of an activity. In Chapter 4 we saw the need to develop research skills, not simply the skill of operating a machine:

> The children pick it up quicker than most teachers, but they need to be aware of the need for teaching research strategies to the children.
>
> (Hampshire teacher)

The key point, as another teacher pointed out, 'is how to *use* the information, rather than simply print it out'. This relationship between computer skills and the curriculum is a general concern. For example, in using *Directions 2000* it was easy to become over-impressed with the speed and confidence with which students started using the recording facility on the disc. It took a little time to focus on the important questions for the language teacher: 'Does the disc help students learn new vocabulary and did the recording activity help their pronunciation?'

Teachers have an important role to play in seeing that computers are used to support the curriculum and that the development of computer skills is not seen as an end in itself. This implies a need for structured support for learning, but some teachers see a tension between providing a structure and giving children the opportunity to explore. As a teacher in Kent points out, children also learn by experimenting with the technology, 'allowing the children to "play" with the machine and find out what they want could be more beneficial than being prescriptive about its uses'.

As with other forms of IT, teachers also have concerns over equality of access. The problem begins with the difficulty of organising access to ensure maximum availability and use. This is particularly difficult in schools with few CD-ROM systems.

> We only have one system in our school. We are considering restricting it to a particular topic and/or age group in order to allow maximum usage and entitlement for all. We have found that the system is popular and all too easily hijacked by enthusiasts.
>
> (Hampshire headteacher)

It is a superb medium for children to use because it generates interest and excitement and is so versatile in what it can provide. The difficulty can be ensuring enough children get hands-on experience.

(Devon middle school teacher)

Schools have adopted a number of strategies for increasing support for pupils, including a form of peer tutoring and parental support.

Find good tutor/mentors from the upper classes in your school who can be given responsibility for teaching the younger ones. Once the children are familiar, then the staff will realise its potential. Often the most interested children are the clever and/or 'difficult' boys!

CD-ROMs are definitely a positive feature and tool in a 'developing' forward moving classroom; however, to use them to their full advantage assistance for the children in the form of an experienced NTA or parent helper is essential.

(Humberside teacher)

THE QUALITY AND RANGE OF SOFTWARE

One of the features of multimedia technology is that it provides easy access to a wealth of information through a wide range of special effects including animation, video and sound. However, these effects are regarded as something of a mixed blessing by many teachers. On the one hand, teachers are aware that software without sophisticated special effects is likely to appear dull and uninteresting to a generation of learners brought up with computers at home and software created to appeal to the home market. As a teacher from Cheshire remarked, 'Video clips are now essential. Expectations have risen dramatically, and children are disappointed if things don't move/speak/dance, etc.!' In the eyes of this teacher, software used in school has to be seen to be at least as interesting as that which is available at home, but attractive special effects should not be the only criterion for selection of software. One Derbyshire teacher cautioned his colleagues to look beyond 'the excellent special effects and consider the real educational value of the discs'. For him that meant considering the cost and availability of discs relevant to the National Curriculum.

While there is an ever-increasing amount of software coming on to the market, teachers are aware of large gaps in provision for both young children and older less able learners. Apart from the 'talking books' there is still precious little available for infants and young children.

The software could be improved by a greater selection for infants. Infant children in our experience can become adept very quickly at using the CD-ROMs especially when finding out information, only to find that the information is pitched above them.

(Sunderland infant teacher)

In addition some infants experience co-ordination difficulties in using the mouse and may benefit from age-appropriate programs which can be operated from the keyboard.

Multimedia technology has proved to be of particular value for learners of all ages with special educational needs.

> It has allowed them a greater access to information and graphics that are not available with other technology. Learners with special educational needs are also able to set the computer up themselves.
>
> (Northumberland teacher)

However, despite these advantages, there needs to be more thought given to software provision for pupils with special educational needs, especially at Key Stages 3 and 4. Sceptics might argue that such software is unlikely to have a high priority in an industry dominated by the relatively profitable home market.

Teachers' perceptions of what was available for individual subject areas were coloured by their difficulties in getting access to discs. Many teachers told us that they knew that there were more and more titles coming on to the market but they simply did not have the time to look at them. They were frustrated that in many cases they could not order inspection copies, as they could with books, and were perplexed over the pricing of discs. They were worried about ordering something which would not give value for money.

As we have seen in Chapter 5, there was growing concern that software manufacturers should develop close links with British teachers and educationalists 'as the potential is so great and should not be driven by the home market or USA'.

> The potential of CD-ROM is *huge*: but the discs are mainly *given* to us rather than generated by teachers' needs. There is massive scope for classroom use of multimedia discs if those discs could better serve what we really needed. For instance *Encarta*, though wonderful, is *too* complex in some ways. *Living Stories* are wonderful but *Just Grandma and Me* is unavailable as a book! These discs, though wonderful, have just been plonked down on schools.
>
> (Tower Hamlets primary teacher)

In time we would expect the market to settle down and for publishers to respond more sympathetically to teachers' needs. We would also expect costs of discs to fall with technological improvements and in response to an expanding market. Teachers are often disappointed in the software which is currently available. 'There is a lot of rubbish on the market!' (Devon primary teacher). Even potentially useful software is found to be disappointing because the language is too difficult or it is difficult to integrate it into existing programmes of study. Organisation of material is also seen as important:

Remember children explore and press every box/window. For some discs – ensure the pathways are clear and logical for a child's progress into and exiting from the disc's programs.

(Northants junior teacher)

Similarly, teachers are likely to be looking for software which offers a high level of interactivity, including facilities such as integrated word processing and printing.

Worries over curriculum relevance

As the wealth of CD-ROMs produced for the home market demonstrates, learners of all ages find multimedia software interesting and enjoyable to use. In schools multimedia technology has proven so popular that sessions on the CD-ROM have been used as rewards for good behaviour or for use in a computer club. However, there is a growing awareness that using the technology as an amusement or a hobby is to deny its potential as a tool for learning. Increasingly teachers are trying to find ways of using the technology to support learning in all aspects of the curriculum. This necessitates a shift in perspective.

Teachers should not treat a session on the machine as a prize or a toy. They should emphasise it is just another tool and discourage children from using it to 'play' without direction. The discs can be used in ways which distinguish them from adventure and other computer games and this needs to be made clear to pupils and staff.

(Southwark teacher)

Teachers perceive a need for whole school policies for all aspects of IT to ensure continuity and progression. Such policies also help to support enthusiastic staff and ensure maximum use of the machines. Some teachers would find it helpful to have a model to follow when drawing up a school policy incorporating the use of CD-ROMs, particularly in relation to OFSTED expectations. In the absence of such a model, the advice from teachers is to work from existing practice in schools. 'You must seek to make your products fit the curriculum needs of schools, not the other way around' (Cheshire primary teacher). Meanwhile a Norfolk teacher identifies a need for 'examples of the use of CD-ROM discs in an ordinary classroom – with reference to the relevant National Curriculum references and ideas or topics worksheets, etc.'. A recurring theme of this book is the tension caused by the teacher's concern for a close curriculum fit and the exploratory nature of much of multimedia software.

Teachers are divided on the way in which to develop National Curriculum links. Some want to see the development of quite closely targeted software to support particular aspects of their teaching. For example, a Devon teacher wanted software specifically on the Tudors and Stuarts or Columbus which would have direct links with those aspects of the history curriculum. Other teachers argued against subject-specific software on the grounds that it would be used intermittently and therefore not be cost effective. For example, an IT co-ordinator in a secondary school explained how *Encarta* could be used for topics in history and geography teaching, for statistical investigations in maths (e.g. investigate gender bias in the selection of entries) and for developing writing skills in English (e.g. prepare your own entry for *Encarta*).

TEACHERS AND HOME COMPUTERS

The use of multimedia systems at home is a significant factor in encouraging its use in schools. There are obvious positive aspects to this home–school liaison: competent kids appear in the classroom – a sort of 'child expert' or (as we discussed) an unpaid technician. The presence of a multimedia system may provide pupils with greater motivation to do homework. The system at home may provide the background knowledge or spark to make learning more meaningful in the classroom. Many teachers told us that experiences and interests of children actually drive the introduction of multimedia in their schools.

But some teachers were concerned about aspects of home use. They may feel vulnerable with the 'classroom expert'; 'cheating' may occur with the child who uses a multimedia system for homework, using huge, unfiltered chunks printed straight from *Encarta* (but, as other teachers asked, is this different from copying from a printed book?). Losing control may also be a worry if the student is seen as a subject expert, say on the human body, as a result of using one of the many discs on human anatomy, or on the solar system, the Second World War, or many other topics. The introduction of multimedia may threaten to undermine the teacher's authority (both as 'an authority', i.e. a 'subject expert', and as someone 'in authority', i.e. with discipline over a class: Peters 1966).

The implications of home use – and they have yet to be realised in both senses of the word – are enormous for the teacher's role, expectations and position of authority. We finish this section by showing an exaggerated version of the contrasts between home (or informal) learning and school (formal) learning. The box is not meant in any way to devalue the work of teachers in the school context, and the descriptions do not always apply. It is simply intended to present, in a stark way, some of the differences between learning in the two contexts.

HOME LEARNING/INFORMAL (Other than 'homework')	SCHOOL LEARNING/ FORMAL
voluntary	compulsory
haphazard, unstructured, unsequenced	structured and sequenced
open-ended	often more closed, goal-directed
non-assessed, not certificated	assessed, certificated
informal setting	classroom- and institution-based
unplanned	planned
learner-led, learner-centred	often teacher-led, teacher-centred
many unintended outcomes (outcomes more difficult to measure)	fewer unintended outcomes
undirected, not legislated for	legislated and directed, controlled
low 'currency'	high 'currency'

SUMMARY

We must regard teacher development and teacher attitude as vitally important parts in the equation leading to 'effective IT use'. But the picture is complicated – we cannot assume crude 'deficit models' of teachers and simply blame them. We must look at the institution as a whole (as we do in Chapter 7) and the general picture of hardware, software, school management, the curriculum and the fabric and layout of the school – the equation is a complex one.

Professional development has several components. As one teacher put it, there is a kind of 'learning cycle' or equation in IT which requires the right mixing and timing of several elements: INSET, staff time for experience and reflection, technical support, and availability of hardware and software. These ingredients, correctly timed, are all needed in order for progress in IT use to take place (Scaife and Wellington 1993: 96).

There are at least three important practical points which can be distilled from this chapter. First, people learn about IT socially – there are often 'super users', adult or child, in a school (or at home) who are valuable in this process and the social use of IT may drive its use in school. The second point is to affirm the need for training and professional development, in particular for training programmes or events which focus on 'how to do the job better' (Clegg 1994), rather than the technology and how to operate it. The management of people and their attitudes is as important as the management of resources. Indeed, the people of an institution like a school are its most expensive and its most valuable resource. As this quote illustrates, teachers' and indeed pupils' attitudes to technology are often modified or changed by access to the technology itself; in addition to special events, teachers need time to reflect on classroom experiences:

I find the CD-ROM has profoundly changed my perception of IT. In our school it has generated great enthusiasm and interest among both staff and pupils. *Encarta, Dinosaurs, Musical Instruments* and *Anglo-Saxons* have all been used to support and enrich topic work in both key stages.

(Cheshire primary teacher)

Thus, just as teachers can influence IT use in their schools, the use of IT can affect teachers. Our third point in this summary is to draw attention yet again to the software and the curriculum. Teachers can begin to address this mismatch only by a virtuous cycle of accommodation and assimilation in which the use of multimedia is used not only to support the existing curriculum but also in time to change it. Olson (1988) for example has suggested that computer use affects both teachers and pupils. He argues that teachers often use computers to express things about their own practice – to make a personal statement. As a result, through using IT teachers may be encouraged, or even forced, to

● rethink what they teach
● rethink their role and their methods, i.e. how they teach
● rethink their values, i.e. why they teach.

Olson goes further by arguing that IT use can also enable pupils to look critically at what they are learning, how they learn it and why. This may become especially true with the spread of multimedia systems into the home. This in turn may pose a challenge to teachers and to the curriculum, possibly to schooling itself.

However, these changes must take place within the context of an institution with all its influence, history and inertia – this is the subject of the next chapter.

Chapter 7

Multimedia in schools

Having examined some of the issues concerning the professional development of teachers, we turn to the development of institutions. Here we explore
the potential of the multimedia technology and examine the institutional
factors that inhibit the impact of the technology on teaching and learning.
In particular we address the practical and pedagogical issues that face teachers
when they wish to use multimedia technology as a learning tool. Multimedia
seems to provide opportunities for a more learner-centred approach in school
but why is such an approach so difficult to implement? We look at issues
of control, classroom management and the recurring problems of curriculum
fit. We then examine the introduction of CD-ROM systems into schools
and decisions that schools have taken on where to put the computer.

We begin by considering the general issues as they apply to primary and
secondary schools, noting that some are common to both sectors while others
are more prominent in one than the other. Later we present separate primary
and secondary case studies which illustrate different approaches schools have
taken to the organisation of resources.

THE TECHNOLOGICAL POTENTIAL

The introduction of multimedia into schools is seen by many as an important step in a 'technological revolution'.

> Revolution may seem a strong word to describe the advent of 'educational
> computing'. It isn't. Nothing before has so stirred schools into action.
> School systems, teachers, parents and children talk about computers as
> they never talked about programmed learning, educational television, open
> learning nor raising the school leaving age, for that matter.
>
> (Olson 1988: 1)

If we are going to use the term 'educational revolution' to describe the impact
of multimedia it has got to refer to important changes in approaches to teaching and learning and not simply the particular means by which material is
produced. Like many of the tools available in modern classrooms, multimedia

technology could be seen as a neutral resource able to support a full range of teaching and learning styles. For example, Olson goes on to note:

> the computer can act as an educational learning aid, much as a text does, giving drill and practice and tutoring students in a variety of subjects. The teacher teaches by directing what and how the student learns by deliberately selecting appropriate software or other resources according to certain intentions.
>
> (Olson 1988: 2)

But multimedia technology has the potential to be much more than a personal tutor; many of the discs we have looked at seek to change not only the way in which pupils access and use information both in school and at home but also their relationship to the material. Relatively easy access to vast amounts of data offers pupils of all ages the opportunity to become independent learners and take control of their learning. For example, when writing about the potential of computers in education, Walker and Hess (1984) cited 'individual tailored learning, independent learning, and more active learning'. This suggests an image of motivated pupils following their own independent lines of inquiry with the teacher on hand to provide appropriate guidance and support. However, in the past schools have often been unable or unwilling to exploit the full potential of the technology. It is often said that someone returning from outer space and walking into a secondary school classroom would observe that little has changed since the mid-1940s. Similarly, if all the computers in a school used for teaching and learning (as opposed to administration) were to 'go down' on a given day there would be virtually no impact on school life. It is interesting to contrast this observation with the situation when computers 'go down' in (say) banking, retail or the travel industry. So why is this?

The image of child-centred learning is not new. There have been a number of attempts to introduce an educational system which is based on a respectful attitude to learners and a democratic social philosophy.

> For example, John Dewey's idea that children would learn better if learning were truly a part of living experience; or Freire's idea that they would learn better if they were truly in charge of their own learning processes; or Jean Piaget's idea that intelligence emerges from an evolutionary process in which many factors must have time to find their equilibrium; or Lev Vygotsky's idea that conversation plays a crucial role in learning.
>
> (Papert 1993: 15)

What these disparate innovations have in common is that they all, in their various ways, attempt to put the learner at the centre of the educational process. However, while they have all had, and continue to have, support from different aspects of the educational establishment they have all failed to bring about radical change. There is some disagreement about the reasons for this. Papert, for example, blames the education establishment, including most of its research community, which he sees as remaining

> largely committed to the educational philosophy of the late nineteenth and early twentieth centuries, and so far none of those who challenge these hallowed traditions has been able to loosen the hold of the educational establishment on how children are taught.
>
> (Papert 1993: 3)

Our review tracing past attempts at introducing IT into schools shows that Papert is wide of the mark at least in the UK context. There has been no shortage of innovatory projects associated with IT and a commitment to the use of 'emancipatory software' in schools. Instead, we believe that the real difficulty lies in the potential conflict between so-called 'progressive' teaching approaches and delivering a prescribed curriculum to large classes with scarce resources. The teacher who wishes to support open-ended child-centred learning faces a serious dilemma. Little wonder that many teachers resolve this dilemma by using the technology to 'add to existing practice rather than replace it' (Latchem *et al.* 1993: 28).

THE TEACHER'S DILEMMA

Macfarlane (1997) talks abut the 'teacher's dilemma' by referring to a conflict between the culture of the classroom and the culture of the computer. Multimedia gives learners the power to explore and manipulate information, and enable individuals to construct their own 'knowledge base'. In contrast, present institutional demands on teachers ensure that the culture of the classroom is governed by the need to control learning outcomes, to maintain authority, to meet the demands of content-laden syllabi, and at the same time moderate the behaviour of a large group of young people. The strategies that teachers have necessarily developed for achieving the latter set of aims have clashed with their role in allowing or even nurturing the independence of the learner. As Tyack and Cuban (1995: 83) put it, 'computer meets classroom – classroom wins'.

Few people would doubt the value of multimedia systems in teaching and learning. If one observes students of any age working with them (including one's own children) their potential for active learning, exploration and motivation is apparent. Yet when this marvellous platform for learning meets the institution, strange things can happen. Again, to quote Tyack and Cuban (1995: 83), 'some innovations seem to die on contact with the institutional reality of the school'. Rather than schools and teaching patterns *accommodating* the reform, the innovation becomes '*assimilated* to previous patterns of schooling' (Tyack and Cuban 1995: 83, original emphasis).

Even when resource levels for multimedia become high, we need to recognise the trends since the late nineteenth century which Tyack and Cuban have so clearly pointed out. Teachers will continue to use technologies that 'fit familiar routines and classroom procedures'. They use technologies which 'enhance their regular instruction but rarely to transform their teaching' (Tyack and Cuban 1995: 122). This is understandable given the management, curricular and societal constraints within which they work. The classroom itself has proved to be the hardest thing to change. We wonder what our alien from outer space will observe when returning fifty years hence. Will the institution still have the upper hand?

CONTROL, OWNERSHIP AND TEACHER INTERVENTION

Key issues for teaching and learning in the school context include the difficult business of control and ownership. Teachers are certainly discouraged (by the pressures of the National Curriculum and OFSTED for example) to relinquish control over children's learning. But their own perspective on the teacher's role is also important. Fox (1983) presents four metaphors or 'theories of teaching' which teachers may follow.

> There is the transfer theory which treats knowledge as a commodity to be transferred from one vessel to another. There is the shaping theory which treats teaching as a process of shaping or moulding students to a predetermined pattern. Thirdly, there is the travelling theory which treats a subject as a terrain to be explored with hills to be climbed for better viewpoints with the teacher as the travelling companion or expert guide. Finally, there is a growing theory which focuses more attention on the intellectual and emotional development of the learner.
>
> (Fox 1983: 151)

In our opinion travelling or growing theories of teaching and learning are likely to lead to the kind of independent learning, open-ended activity and flexible curriculum which computers in general, and multimedia technology in particular, are best able to support. Teachers who believe their task is to guide or support pupils are also likely to hold the view that knowledge is individually constructed through negotiation with others. Such teachers believe there is a need to identify specific learning outcomes for children and have a clear plan of the skills or concepts to be learned – this is not the same at all as the *laissez-faire* approach favoured by so-called 'progressive' teachers. However, they are also aware of the need to be alert to the fluctuating needs of individual pupils. In contrast the discourse of the National Curriculum – we talk about delivering the curriculum almost as if we were delivering parcels of goods – fits much more closely towards transfer or shaping theories of learning which many innovations within IT have not been designed to support.

These issues of supervision and teacher intervention are also crucial in considering how multimedia is to be used in schools. We saw that in earlier studies of IV use (e.g. NCET 1994d) teachers were prepared to allow un-supervised use of multimedia, but still wanted to intervene by imposing some structure on it, e.g. time limits or guided activity (worksheets). The instance we found of a banda sheet being used to structure and guide pupils' use of a CD-ROM may not be uncommon. We are not arguing against structured learning as such; we saw in Chapter 4 the importance of guided tasks in intro-ducing research strategies and encouraging purposeful use. The 'teacher's dilemma' is to set structured but open-ended tasks and at the same time encourage pupils to take control of their learning. Resolving this dilemma has been further problematised by the introduction of the National Curriculum.

Many teachers want to use CD-ROM software to help them teach the National Curriculum, and many express a need for more information and guidance that would help them do so. This is a perfectly reasonable request but will publishers respond by producing linear, tightly structured learning material? Perhaps it is too early to say. Some teachers made it clear that they were at a very early stage in this process of integration:

> So I think basically we are still at the stage of getting everybody familiar with the hardware, how to use the CD-ROM, getting around a program. . . . At the moment children are handing on their knowledge to each other and teachers are just supervising the children and just checking that they have a right idea.
>
> (Sheffield teacher)

CLASSROOM MANAGEMENT

Along with worries over curriculum 'fit', classroom management of IT is, understandably, to the forefront in teachers' minds. Where should the machines be situated and how should they be used (Figure 7.1)? Should teachers go for whole-class teaching (often called the 'electronic blackboard mode'), group activities (the 'computer in the corner mode') or individu-alised learning (the 'battery-hen mode')?

We have seen a number of lessons in which the teacher has chosen to use the technology as the basis for whole-class lessons or discussions. In one class-room, poetry software was used regularly as a shared reading activity. In another classroom the teacher used encyclopedia software to lead the class through 'a journey round the world'. In both classes the shared activity was seen as an important way to teach specific IT skills and often provided an interesting introduction to subsequent small-group activities. However, as Chapter 6 identified, in primary schools computers are predominantly used in pairs or in small groups. Where computers are outside the classroom in shared areas pupils often work largely unsupervised; in these circumstances 'peer tutoring' is seen as a popular and effective strategy for supporting pupil use of the technology.

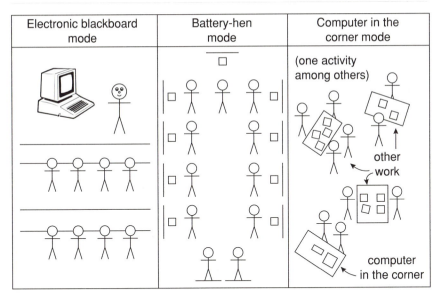

Electronic blackboard mode	Battery-hen mode	Computer in the corner mode

Figure 7.1 Ways of using multimedia in the classroom

ORGANISATIONAL ISSUES

Schools differ considerably in the kind and number of machines they have. Some schools are so well equipped that they have new high powered computers in each classroom, with additional machines in shared resource areas or the school library. Other schools are noticeably less well off and a shortage of equipment means that classes are forced to share machines that often fall short of the specification teachers would like. The frustration that teachers feel at having to make do with old and unreliable machines was summarised by one teacher.

> One of the problems is that many of our computers are ageing and a lot of them were fairly crummy to start with. Just getting them set up and getting them going is time consuming and enough to put a lot of teachers off.
>
> (Milton Keynes teacher)

All the teachers we spoke to wanted to see an increase in the amount and specification of the technology available in schools. Keeping up with developments in technology is seen as important by pupils, parents and teachers. This is especially significant given the number of pupils who had access to technology at home.

> The kids found the CD-ROM videos fascinating. They thought it was great because they are not used to seeing things like that on school

computers. They have all this wonderful technology at home; what we offer at school has to be more dynamic for them.

(Sheffield teacher)

Many teachers also wanted to see equitable provision of computers in schools with a greater attempt to raise the baseline of provision. This would require fundamental changes in central resourcing and an approach that positively discriminates in favour of schools with limited resources.

Despite discrepancies in provision, the majority of schools have one or more machines which are shared between classes. Schools have coped with this situation by adopting one of a range of strategies which we characterise as classroom based (where the machine is located in one classroom but may be accessed by other pupils); mobile machine (where the machine is physically moved between classrooms); and central location (where the machine is based in a shared area such as a library or computer room) (see NCET 1996 for further details).

Schools seem to adopt the strategy that they believe ensures maximum use of the technology and/or the most equitable access for pupils. Any strategy has advantages and disadvantages, and consequences that reach into the classrooms themselves. The important principle is that schools have a coherent and thought-through policy linking organisational issues at both school and classroom level. For example, decisions about location have affected the ease with which teachers involved with whole classes can monitor the activities of children working on the CD-ROM, and the ease with which children can ask for help from teachers in case of difficulty. On the basis of their experience so far, teachers often made comments like 'it is vital to plan for good access'. However, teachers are often limited in the amount of time they can devote to supporting children using computers.

In reality, a school's approach is often determined by practicalities; for instance, in one school the system was placed in a shared area only because classrooms were too full to hold it. Another school was in a two-storey building:

In a school like this which is on two levels it's actually been quite a job administering it, which is part of my role. And of course shifting [the system] up and down is not ideal. So that's a problem with it, but what it does mean is that every class throughout the school gets access to it. We had considered whether to base it in the library and use it as a library-based resource, but we felt that the people who were furthest away, basically our infant department, and some of our junior classes, would not benefit because it would not be easy to supervise. You wouldn't want a whole class of children in our library area, and it would not be easy to supervise between the two places. If we had more [classroom] support perhaps that would be a possibility.

(IT co-ordinator)

In large secondary schools, logistics plays a vital role too: split sites, stairs, subject blocks and separate buildings are key factors.

The constraints on the curriculum were summarised by Taylor *et al.* (1974); these are still applicable in the late 1990s (see box).

SET A: CONSTRAINTS IMPOSED BY THE HUMAN ELEMENT
(PERSONAL)

Subset 1   a Level of enthusiasm of staff
             b Readiness of staff to give time to preparing work both in and out of school
             c General leadership within the school
             d Level of professional training of teachers
             e Level of provision for in-service training, e.g. time off to attend courses, courses available
             f My own level of competence as a teacher
Subset 2   a Quality of caretaking and cleaning staff
             b Level of provision of clerical help
             c Level of provision of ancillary classroom help

SET B: ORGANISATIONAL AND ADMINISTRATIVE CONSTRAINTS

Subset 1   a Form of class organisation existing in school, e.g. free/traditional, vertical grouping, etc.
             b Adequacy of communication of what one is to teach, e.g. through syllabus, schemes of work, etc.
             c Style of discipline in the school
             d Form of timetable, e.g. laid down, free work, etc.
             e Range of school activities, e.g. plays, clubs, sports, etc.
Subset 2   a Liaison between schools (e.g. infant/junior) or between staff within schools
             b Number of children per class
             c Age of children
             d Children's previous experience of being taught
             e Socio-economic linguistic background, i.e. home environment
Subset 3   a Style of local education authority administration
             b Form of government educational policy
             c Level of provision of consumable materials
             d Level of financial provision

SET C: PHYSICAL CONSTRAINTS

             a Size and design of classrooms
             b Level of provision of storage space
             c Number of classrooms
             d Specialist facilities, e.g. music room, laboratory etc.
             e Form and style of school architecture

Source: Taylor *et al.* (1974: 22)

CASE STUDIES

The short accounts which follow paint a picture of the state of multimedia use in several English schools or colleges in 1996. The institutions were chosen because they reflect different patterns of use. What they have in common is that they offered access and indeed welcomed an outsider being there to 'see what was happening', to talk things over with them, and perhaps to offer some advice. We would not pretend that they are a representative sample – they are 'snapshots' of schools which are used to illustrate several points. For example, resource levels for multimedia (hardware and software) in all the cases are still extremely low and this must be a major factor in inhibiting its use. But the case studies illustrate several issues not connected to resource levels, some of which have been discussed at other points in the book:

1 *The dominance of the curriculum and the need for curriculum 'fit'*: for example, flexible use of multimedia is made difficult by, particularly in secondary schools, the 'height' of subject boundaries, and, on a more day-to-day level, the need to fit multimedia use into timed and timetabled lessons and to schemes of work (sometimes slavishly followed for good practical reasons). The need for IT to 'fit the curriculum' was apparent in all the schools studied, and has been widely reported in earlier studies (e.g. for IV see NCET 1994d).

2 *Classroom and school organisation*: how does multimedia fit into the typical classroom? Should computers come to the class (on a trolley) or should classes go to the computer room? Should small groups, or even whole classes, go to the library during lesson time? (In one secondary example, students were sent out of lessons using a study permit signed by the class teacher to work in the library.) Could students use computers during breaks and before/after school hours? How should home use of multimedia be catered for and encouraged? The case studies also illustrate the importance of the logistics of the school: split sites, stairs, subject blocks and separate buildings – what influence do these have on multimedia use?

3 *Control of learning*: can or will teachers (especially the subject specialists of secondary education) relinquish control over children's learning? How do teachers offer guidance, supervision and intervention when children learn with multimedia?

4 *Teacher 'development' and teacher attitude:* these are crucial factors and must be considered carefully (see Chapter 6). This includes IT co-ordinators' attitudes towards different types of computers and consequent choices of routes to follow, e.g. the 'Acorn man' in one school studied.

Primary case study 1: classroom-based machine

Corrie Dell is a new primary school serving an affluent area of a city in the south-west of England. It has over 300 pupils aged 4–11. The school is extremely well resourced and has four CD-ROM systems, one of which is located in the shared library area with the others being located in each of the Year 6 classrooms. The school has bought a wide range of software including some British software that caters especially for primary age children. At the time of writing the staff and children were particularly impressed with *The Eyewitness Encyclopaedia of Science*, *Kingfisher Children's Micropedia* and *Creative Writer*.

The staff at Corrie Dell believe that having a CD-ROM system as a permanent fixture in the classroom allows for more integrated curriculum planning; it should also reduce the novelty value often associated with brief and infrequent access to the technology. Moreover, not having to adhere to a school-wide timetable or rota can also allow greater flexibility and spontaneity. However, even where computers are based in classrooms, patterns of use depend, at least in part, on the interest and expertise of the class teacher. Where teachers lack interest, expertise or organisational skills there is a danger that computers could lie idle for long periods of time. While this is not a problem in itself, for example, mathematical equipment is rarely used all day every day, it may be difficult to justify buying expensive equipment for occasional use.

The teacher of one Year 6 class was convinced of the benefit of having the technology available in his room: engaging children in the process of searching for information was more important than the specific content of the search or its relationship to other curriculum work. He said that children should be encouraged to see the CD-ROM as 'just another source of information alongside books, etc.', and consequently he designed activities that were intended to develop children's skills in accessing information. Many of these searches were related to the current class topic.

Primary case study 2: a mobile machine

Penn House Primary School is close to the centre of a city in northern England, and caters for over 200 pupils aged 4–10. The school is surrounded by high-rise flats occupied by working-class families or students (including a significant number of students from abroad). The school has a significant proportion of bilingual pupils and pupils who are just beginning to learn English. It also has a unit catering for children with emotional and behavioural difficulties. The majority of the children in the school are considered by the staff to have special educational needs. Over 80 per cent of the pupils are entitled to free school meals.

The school has one Acorn CD-ROM system which is moved on a trolley from class to class on a rota system. This approach was adopted because the staff feel that it produces maximum access and use. Locating the machine in the classroom provides access for all children, and does not favour those who were felt to be old enough and/or trustworthy enough to work unsupervised in the school library. Moreover, having the machine in the class-room makes it easier for teachers to support learning and monitor pupil progress.

The rota system allows each class to have access to the machine for approximately half a term at a time. However, moving the machine from class to class on a regular basis produces some practical and pedagogical difficulties. On a practical level, the CD-ROM system is not designed to be moved around easily and staff are concerned that the machines are vulnerable, especially when being moved up and down stairs in a split-level site. Moreover, few classrooms have sufficient space to house the computer comfortably. In many cases the solution is to place the computer outside the classroom in a communal shared area. As these areas can be rather noisy, speakers have to be used.

Having worked with the machine for some time the staff feel that moving the machine from class to class ensures that the technology was used. It is difficult, if not impossible, to ignore the computer when it arrives in your room. However, the relatively short timescale has prevented some teachers from really 'getting to grips with the technology and incorporating it into termly planning'. In addition, having the machine outside the classroom reduced the level of input from the teacher. Invariably children are left to work unsupervised while the teacher concentrates on the rest of the class.

In the first year of using the machine all classes had access to talking books with some of the older children being introduced to multimedia encyclopedias.

Not surprisingly, the school would like the resources to buy more machines and to be in a position to have one in every classroom. Present thinking is that the age and ability of the pupils and the layout of the school make it unlikely that additional machines would be used in the library or central resource area.

Primary case study 3: centrally located machines

Redmill Junior School is located on an estate of mainly local authority hous-ing, some miles from the centre of a city in the Midlands. The area is one of high unemployment, with about half of the 200 or so children (aged 7–11) being entitled to free school meals. At the time of writing Redmill had two Acorn CD-ROM systems which were located in a large open area, along with several other computers, the school library, and facilities for art and crafts.

Locating the CD-ROM systems in the shared area is in keeping with the school's ethos of sharing resources and of encouraging children to become independent learners. In addition the staff assume that locating the system in the library leads children and teachers to integrate their use of technology with more traditional print-based materials. A rota system ensures that each class has access to the computers. This timetabled access allows teachers to plan their classes' use of the technology.

Situating the computer outside the classroom can create problems for teachers wanting to support and monitor learning. At Redmill they have tried to overcome these difficulties by establishing an interesting model for 'cascading' expertise in using CD-ROM through the school. When the machines first arrived, twelve Year 6 pupils were chosen as 'CD monitors' and trained by the IT co-ordinator for the school. These monitors began by training the rest of the class and then went on to train pupils in Year 5. Each monitor has a day timetabled each week when they work with children of various years on the CD-ROM.

The potential difficulties of using peer tutors (see Chapter 6) is illustrated in the following account of two Year 3 children working with a monitor. The aim of their reading of a talking book was to help the development of their IT skills and reading. Josie (the monitor) helped them start by clicking through the first story with the mouse. She said very little in terms of describing what she was doing (other than 'You click here' a few times) but the younger children watched her as she moved the cursor on the screen. She did not ask them to read the story out loud. Having reached the end, she asked them which other story from the menu they would like to read. This led to some argument: neither child seemed to wish to take responsibility for choosing and Brian was not an enthusiastic participant at this stage. Eventually, Jean asked Josie to pick another story, and Brian took over the mouse to take them through it. He did this confidently and effectively, making only one error (inadvertently returning to the beginning of the story) which Josie was easily able to sort out.

While they were reading the second story, another CD monitor (Alan, 11 years old) came over and told Brian and Jean that they ought to be reading the story first and then using the 'voice' as a check. They continued and then went on to read (i.e. watch and listen to) a third story. This was chosen by Brian while Jean operated the mouse. The use of the mouse was not explicitly negotiated, but never seemed at all contentious.

Our observations (on this and other activities at Redmill) provide strong support for the value of the CD monitor system as a way of sharing IT expertise among children. However, they also suggest that teachers need to identify effective strategies for peer support and make those strategies explicit.

Secondary case study 1: the learning resource centre

Town High School is a 14–18 college, with 1,500 students and a thirty-form entry, on the edge of a medium-sized town, eight miles from a large city.

The college has two new multimedia systems (one with an Internet connection) in the library (which they called the learning resource centre or LRC), one system in a resource room in science and one on a trolley in the science department (all are PC systems).

The library has an excellent, well-organised collection of discs – the covers were on display in their cases and students can then ask for the actual disc they wanted from 'behind the counter (Virgin megastore style)', using their personal card with a bar-code on it.

The science department was building up its own collection of discs and had *Elements, New Scientist, Materials, Earth and Universe*. One teacher (who had her own multimedia system at home) had bought three science discs out of her own pocket – she 'likes to have them herself so that she knows them and is not frightened of them'.

Year 12 and 13 pupils were commonly using discs such as *Encarta* and *New Scientist* to do research for assignments. For example, Year 13 students were looking up the terms 'cystic fibrosis' and 'gene therapy' for an essay on genetics for A-level Biology. Two Year 11 pupils were using *Encarta* to help with their science revision for the General Certificate of Secondary Education (GCSE), searching (quite successfully) on a range of topics including pollution, the carbon cycle, and the human body. This took place in the library (LRC) with little supervision. The teacher simply gave them a list of topics to look up and sent them to the LRC from her teaching lab for a fifty minute lesson.

One science teacher was observed using a multimedia system with the disc *Earth and Universe* on a trolley in her lab as part of a revision lesson on the solar system. Pupils were working in twos and threes, without a worksheet, for around ten minutes – thus four groups were able to use the resources in a fifty minute period.

One teacher commented on the current 'one disc to each machine' problem and suggested that suppliers should sell multiple copies of compact discs with the second, third, fourth, etc., at a reduced price. A lunch-time discussion over coffee included an informal chat about what discs were now in the school, what their content was and how people had used them. One teacher felt that this kind of sharing was vital and worthy of prime staff development time. One of the 'unconvinced' said:

> If I had a multimedia system in my room I'd use it, just like any other resource. But I wouldn't go out of my way to use multimedia. I wouldn't take the kids to a special room. It's easier to use books and other resources that are on hand.

Secondary case study 2: mixed modes of use

Garforth Community College is an 11–18 comprehensive with 1,800 on roll and a ten-form entry. It is situated on a large site in the suburbs of a major city.

Its resources are typical for an establishment of this size. It has two PC multimedia stations in the library, one of which is 'on loan' from the business studies department. The college also has three Acorn multimedia systems, one is situated in the science department, one in technology, and the other in what is termed the 'support department'. The latter is designated for the use of special educational needs pupils in the main part of the school. In addition the sixth form block has three multimedia systems (two PCs and an Acorn). The college's selection of discs have been acquired either as 'free gifts' with the hardware or as purchases from the library or departmental budgets. Review copies have been donated by one of the teachers who reviews CDs for a teacher's science journal. A single IT technician is employed to support IT across the college in terms of trouble-shooting and general assistance.

There are different modes of use in different departments in the college. For example, discs were used in the library more than anywhere else in the school. Discs in common use were: *Grolier Encyclopaedia*, *Encarta*, *Eyewitness Encyclopaedia*, newspapers on CD such as *The Times* and the *Guardian*, *Dangerous Creatures* and the *History of the World*.

The librarian has established a well-managed system to allow free access to pupils after the end of the school day, as well as access for Year 7 and Year 8 pupils at first break, Year 9 to Year 11 pupils at second break and Year 12 pupils at any time. When demand was great (at most times) she operated a carefully marshalled booking system. In addition, whole classes often used the library; the two multimedia systems were used as part of a carousel of activities. The librarian said that she could 'easily use ten multimedia systems in the library'.

The science department was enthusiastic about its use of CD-ROM. Modes of uses included an 'electronic blackboard' (their term); pupils carrying out their own research as part of a 'circus' of activities (the main difficulty here being the time required for everyone to 'get round' before moving on to a new topic) and as a self-access facility for after-school use.

The department are planning 'teacher-led worksheets' to go with the discs, and are 'beginning to write CD-ROMs into their schemes of work'. They feel that searching the discs is not an easy skill to acquire and therefore needs to be developed. Discs in common use were: *The Interactive Periodic Table*, *Materials* and *The Living World*.

In the support department staff are using the Acorn system to support individual learning for pupils who have been taken out of mainstream classes. Discs like *Speaking Starspell*, *Breakaway Maths* and *Kingfisher Children's Micropedia* were used to support in developing numeracy and literacy skills.

A survey carried out by a teacher revealed that, of a sample of 511 pupils in Years 7 to 9, 80 per cent had computers at home; 107 pupils (21 per cent) had multimedia systems. A further 143 pupils (28 per cent) said they were considering buying a multimedia system for home. The teacher who carried out the survey said: 'It shows that the school is in quite an affluent part of the city.'

The perennial difficulties of lack of resources and lack of time were mentioned, for example finding the time to develop teachers' knowledge of the discs in the college and of what might be available to buy. Teachers were concerned that pupils need to develop skills such as carrying out search strategies but there was some disagreement as to who should be responsible for teaching them. The teachers also worry about 'letting the kids loose', not least because they were fearful of 'losing control over learning outcomes'.

Teachers are now on the verge of being able to set a homework or assignment based on a CD-ROM for a whole class, if the class were given a long enough period to complete it. They are not yet at the stage where homework is set which could rely on the use of multimedia.

Secondary case study 3: getting started in a big school

City Suburb Comprehensive is a large 11–16 comprehensive, with 1,600 on roll and a nine-form entry, spreading over a big site (several separate buildings) on the northern edge of a large city.

The library has its own A5000-based Acorn multimedia system, the staffroom has a PC-based system and there 'will soon be two new Acorn systems on the top floor of the science block' for use in humanities and science. A room on the same floor already houses a PC-based multimedia system used mostly by history and geography departments.

As for future resourcing, there seems to be some conflict or debate between the IT co-ordinator, described as 'an Acorn man', and other staff who would like to 'go down the PC route with multimedia'.

The school was not well supplied with discs – most were in a box in the library (marshalled by the librarian) and were obtained 'by hook and by crook'. Discs such as the *Guardian*, *The Illustrated Works of Shakespeare*, *Space Encyclopaedia* and *Frontier 2000* were held in the box in random order. There did not seem to be a clear system for staff or students to borrow the discs.

Library use was not yet well organised or established – the staff were in the process of setting things up. The humanities department used its multimedia system (which had initially been set up to show satellite images). History and geography discs had been bought out of their own departmental budget (discs such as *Encarta*, Census data, and an atlas).

The physical layout of the school and its departmental management structure were major barriers. The school is on a single site, but it is a large one. One multimedia system was on the top floor of a four-storey building and tended to be confined to humanities use, partly because it was nearby. Science was planning to get its own multimedia system but had five labs on one floor, two on another and two in a separate building. The science staff wondered how they were to deploy it. There is also the practical problem that a single disc could be used on only one machine at a time.

In addition, the school has 'an ethos of high departmental boundaries', as one teacher put it. Co-operation between departments in buying and using discs seemed unlikely – the teacher guessed that there were three copies of *Encarta* somewhere around the school!

The teachers were keen to use multimedia in teaching and learning. They recognised some of the physical, mental and management difficulties which needed to be overcome in a large comprehensive of this kind, with several buildings having several floors, a vertical management structure, and a large staff, some of whom were not convinced of the value of multimedia in teaching.

General points

There are certain recurring features which surfaced in all of the cases studied. Our suggestion is that these are probably common to most schools in Britain and conceivably in other countries. Inevitably, the institution plays a major part in influencing the learning and teaching that go on, and therefore (irrespective of resource levels) certain issues relating to the use of multimedia (and IT in general) will be found in any school. The main issues relate to control of learning; the management of learning and teaching, both in the physical organisation and layout of a school, and the organisation of learners; the influence of the curriculum and existing schemes of work and lesson plans; and the attitude and professional development of teachers.

Our contention is that pedagogy is heavily shaped by the organisational constraints and context in which it occurs. These constraints are physical – the scarcity of machines and organising access to them; and cultural – the approach to teaching and learning which is fostered by high subject boundaries and a centrally controlled curriculum. This is almost a statement of the obvious but is often neglected in assessments of the impact of IT in schooling (as opposed to education) and in some of the wilder claims made for the benefits and potential of multimedia use and IT in general.

These organisational conditions lead to specific questions about multimedia use which teachers are forced to address in practical situations – where should systems be positioned and why? How do, and should, teachers and children learn to use the technology? We have shown how vital these questions are in real settings by considering a number of case studies, which both illustrate the importance of the institution and give actual examples of the steps that teachers are taking to make multimedia use possible. Case studies of primary and secondary schools have been provided to illustrate the differences and similarities in organisational and curriculum issues in the two sectors. Our suggestion would be that primary teachers face many constraints but have fewer organisational, practical and subject barriers than their secondary counterparts. However, there are important similarities between the two sectors and teachers can learn much from understanding other people's experience.

Part IV

Conclusions

Chapter 8

Looking back, looking forward

We have described the introduction of multimedia software in the context of a brief history of IT in education, we have looked at learning with multimedia and we have discussed the attitudes of teachers and the impact of institutions on the way in which software is used. What overall impression does this give about the value of using multimedia to support teaching and learning? At the end of Chapter 2 we asked a series of questions about learners, multimedia software and teachers to which we now return. Do we have any answers to these questions? What future do we see for multimedia within the curriculum?

LEARNING AND MULTIMEDIA

How do learners engage with multimedia? How do learners engage with text in a multimedia environment and what do they learn from images?

We have found three key features within the multimedia discs described in this book which help motivate and sustain the interest of the learner. First, the organisation of the material can give the learner a sense of being in control. In particular, hyper-links allow learners to make choices about the path they take through the material (very often they are dealing with huge amounts of material). Learners can also select between different media (e.g. they can choose to hear a pre-recorded text or to read it) and they can choose the order in which they access material (e.g. they can see a simulation of an electric current before or after reading a text on electricity). Second, within many multimedia discs there are 'tools' that encourage learners to interact with the material, to transform it and 'make it their own'. For example, we have seen the use of a notepad into which text from encyclopedic software can be copied and amended (Chapter 4), graphing tools with science software (Chapter 5), and record and playback facilities within foreign language discs (Chapter 1). Third, and this is hardly a surprise, the moving images within multimedia discs appeal strongly to young people.

We saw in Chapter 5 that images seem to make material accessible to learners – something we explored in the context of access to narrative, concepts and cultures. Images seem to play to young people's strengths and encourage them to make links with other kinds of experiences; this can include television viewing. The use of visual images has been criticised by some as turning education into an entertainment and hence devaluing traditional skills, including print literacy. We do not agree. We simply do not see the use of different media as a zero sum game – for example, we believe that multimedia can help children develop reading skills rather than detract from their importance. As we saw in Chapter 3, talking books can give children a sense of story before tackling paper-based books and they can sustain readers' interests through the use of hot spots to help with difficult words. We point to shortcomings in the software and the way in which it is used but the potential to support reading is clear.

Does motivation arise from pushing buttons or is there something deeper going on?

The key question is not whether multimedia motivates – it clearly does – but what does it motivate children to do? There were many times when it seemed that the discs encouraged learners to play. The discs were used as a reward for getting through work quickly and children used them in an unstructured way. When working together children would talk about what they were doing but this talk rarely went beyond exchange of technical expertise, such as an explanation of how to use the mouse, or a simple commentary on what they had done. However, at other times we were more enthusiastic about what multimedia had motivated children to do. We saw learners motivated to explore material they would not otherwise have tackled; to engage with reading over a period of time; to investigate their own research questions; to make hypotheses about motion and to test them; and to practise speaking French.

The engagement with multimedia material for which we are arguing is one where learners interact with each other as much as the material. The two can, and very frequently do, go together. For example, children talk to each other when they have to make something happen (click on a hot spot, move to a new screen, cut and paste text or whatever). However, we are not so much interested in the number of clicks learners make when they explore material but the quality of their thinking and talking. For example, reaching a single decision, say, over which section of the disc *Macbeth* to go to might lead students to review and articulate their knowledge of the play. In contrast, deciding which hot spots to click within a talking book could require many decisions but ones which may be negotiated through a fairly superficial and non-interactive discussion.

The kind of engagement for which we are arguing comes when children are willing to take responsibility for their learning (e.g. in Chapter 4 pupils had to decide which insects to investigate) and when they can share knowledge and information. We believe it is talk between learners which helps them to assimilate new information in the light of their previous knowledge and which provides the stimulus for extending a topic or inquiry.

SOFTWARE

Do we have ways of categorising multimedia software?

In Chapter 2 we drew attention to an earlier attempt to categorise instructional, modelling, simulation and emancipatory software. Describing what software was designed to do is not the same as saying how it will be used (for example, we quoted the case of the teachers who tried to direct children's use of exploratory learning materials by providing their own highly structured banda sheets). But categorising has advantages. First, it focuses attention on the proposed function of the software in the classroom. Rather than ask a general question, say, 'Are there any discs for teaching Key Stage 3 French?', we could be asking more focused questions: 'What kind of instructional or what kind of emancipatory software is there?'

Second, categorising software might not tell us how it will be used but it can highlight mismatches between software design and use. If some teachers are imposing a predetermined structure on children using exploratory discs, there is something going wrong. So do categories work for multimedia?

In the course of our research we saw examples of software that would seem to fit the categories introduced in Chapter 2. For example, some science discs offer a straightforward exposition of a topic, such as the cause of tides, and are clearly examples of instructional software, as are the drill and practice foreign language teaching programs. In contrast, we saw little that we would identify as modelling or simulation software. Instead the bulk of the material we felt was emancipatory: for example, the encyclopedic discs, which aim to eliminate the labour of searching by hand through reams of paper-based material.

The idea of emancipatory multimedia is intriguing. Sometimes multimedia simply made it easier to access certain types of activities. Many language-learning discs contain material that could be adequately provided using a textbook supported by a tape recorder. It was simply much easier to package the material on a small disc. But in other examples the disc presented material, typically moving images and simulations, that could not be easily provided by other means. Of course many of these images could be provided by video playback machines but only with much reduced accessibility and little opportunity to interact with the material.

In Chapter 2 we saw that the role of emancipatory material is to cut out 'inauthentic' labour. But what is inauthentic is rarely simple. For example, we saw (Chapter 5) that while on-screen science experiments allow students to focus directly on making and testing hypotheses, some teachers are worried that the labour they cut out (setting up experiments) is authentic science.

Whatever the strength or weakness of this observation it reminds us that while multimedia makes it easier to do many things, it is a simulation of what we see as the real thing. For example, it is much easier to buy the disc *Pris sur la vif* than to go to France but it is not the same thing at all and a simulated conversation with a French boy or girl on a CD-ROM is not a real conversation and cannot come near to it. Similarly, when Patrick Moore is explaining the mysteries of the universe, he is talking to a camera and not really talking to you – he can be stopped but you cannot ask him to tailor his remarks for you. Within many discs you click on words in text and you can display or hear definitions, but as we saw, say, with *Heather Hits a Home Run* (p. 36) you cannot ask for those definitions to be rephrased.

For these reasons we are interested in what goes on between learners, teachers and students and not simply the interaction between learner and software. Multimedia software may be empancipatory, even liberating; it may cut out time-consuming and repetitive tasks but it can adapt to the learner only within a restricted range of parameters and there may be contexts in which the simulations offered are an inadequate substitute for the real thing.

Do we need new categories?

We found some value in using existing categories and particular value in the notion of emancipatory software, but we also had difficulties. First many of the discs we looked at worked within more than one paradigm. For example, *Directions 2000* (a disc for learners of French) provides both accuracy practice as well as more exploratory reading and listening; the *World of Number* contains quasi-instructional material, simulation activities and databases of pictures best thought of as emancipatory material. This does not invalidate the idea of categories *per se*, but should make us sensitive to the idea that many discs are designed to work within a mix of learning styles – perhaps we could describe these discs as 'portmanteau' software (Hammond 1995b).

A more important concern, however, was that we saw a lot of material that was perhaps instructional in aim but would be better described as narrative in style. In Chapter 5 we referred not only to story discs such as *The Tortoise and the Hare* or *Macbeth*, but also to other software that sought to engage viewers in a story in the broad sense of the word. This engagement could have a quite conscious instructional intent, for example the *Number Puzzles* disc, but worked within an apprenticeship model – perhaps one that makes use of Frank Smith's (1988) idea that learning is almost effortless when it involves joining a club of fellow learners – rather than a didactic one.

Our use of the word narrative here is in contrast to Heppell (1993) who uses the terms *narrative, interactive* and *participatory* to refer to different types of multimedia software. However, he seems chiefly concerned with the organisation of the material not the teaching and learning paradigm to which it fits. For example, he describes narrative software as organised in a more linear or book-like fashion, while interactive software is characterised by non-linear, hyper-linked material. Participatory software differs from the two previous types as it allows the learner to interact and alter the material. An example he gives of the latter is the disc *Le Carnaval des Animaux*, in which young users can listen to the music of Saint-Saëns and draw their own images inspired by what they hear. This is an interesting perspective but perhaps focuses too much on the strategies and procedures that the designer has used. For example, drill and practice activities may be contained within what Heppell (1993) describes as narrative or interactive software and may quite easily build in some kind of participative function, such as the record and playback features on foreign language learning discs.

WHAT WILL FUTURE MULTIMEDIA LOOK LIKE?

We simply do not know the answer to this question but we can identify challenges. The first is posed by many teachers who want to make software more relevant to the National Curriculum. One response here is to produce much more tightly and hierarchically structured material with a particular UK context. However, such an approach has serious drawbacks. On a simple practical level we doubt if some of the North American-produced software, which some teachers are concerned about, will go away – and despite our concern for cultural identity we wonder whether it should. Many of these discs are simply cheaper and more professionally produced than those we have in the UK. But leaving this aside, our major concern about the idea of National Curriculum software is that it will ignore what multimedia does best – allowing learners to pursue their own path through non-hierarchical material. We would much rather see case studies showing how the software can be used to support themes, and indeed statements of attainment, within the National Curriculum rather than designers organising their material in a prescriptive and hierarchical fashion.

The second challenge facing designers is to take advantage of technological advances to provide a more integrated use of media. In particular, designers will soon be able to provide more extensive and higher-quality images over the Internet or within higher-capacity CD-ROM discs. These images need to be used in conjunction with text and not as an add-on facility as with some of the discs we have seen. We would also like to see designers use recorded speech on some discs to provide a more natural explanation of concepts rather than merely provide a recorded back-up of what is often fairly dense and inaccessible printed text. But perhaps the greatest challenge to multimedia designers is to integrate the use of Internet communications tools within multimedia. For example, we look forward to scenarios in which multimedia presentations will play within one window inside a wider screen, while a different window may contain a video link or e-mail link to tutors and other learners. For example, imagine *Pris sur le vif* running in one window with e-mail links to a school in France running in another, or imagine children studying the idea of economic development through viewing images of Kenya, say, within *Encarta* and then being able to e-mail a school in Nairobi. Communications software of this type might be able to address the non-adaptive nature of existing multimedia which we discussed earlier.

HOW DO TEACHERS LEARN TO USE MULTIMEDIA AND HOW DO THEY INCORPORATE IT INTO THEIR TEACHING?

Teachers were often cautiously optimistic about the use of multimedia but also worried about getting access to discs, the lack of time for reviewing discs, time taken in learning to use software and organising access for children, and, in some cases, the quality and range of software. Above all they were worried about incorporating multimedia into their teaching. We quoted a teacher in Chapter 7:

> So I think basically we are still at the stage of getting everybody familiar with the hardware, how to use the CD-ROM, getting around a program. . . . At the moment children are handing on their knowledge to each other and teachers are just supervising the children and just checking that they have a right idea.

This teacher could be describing the start of a reflective learning cycle. The school has overcome the initial challenge and got started with multimedia. Teachers are now in a position to reflect on its use and make changes in practice in the light of experience. But equally this may be the start of a cul-de-sac. The integration of multimedia may impose too many strains on preferred teaching styles or demand too much of the time available for curriculum planning, there might simply be other, and more pressing, priorities. The multimedia systems might not go away – though it would be an interesting experiment to visit schools and see just how many computers are in use at any one time – but they will be wheeled out as an optional extra.

In Chapter 7 we identified teachers who used 'travelling' or 'growing' metaphors for teaching as more able to integrate open-ended and flexible materials into their teaching. But even these teachers are worried about how such materials fit into the National Curriculum – and for many teachers the National Curriculum seemed to be a shorthand to describe the general constraint of meeting the demands of content-laden syllabi backed up by formal assessment and national testing. However, while there are particular issues associated with the integration of multimedia within the National Curriculum this is part of a general dilemma faced by teachers. We want children to be creative and to have control over their learning, but at the same time we want schools to be accountable for their work and teachers to be an authority in the classroom – to moderate and control the behaviour of a large group of young people. Is there any way of dealing with these conflicting goals?

WHAT ROLE DOES THE TEACHER HAVE IN SUPPORTING LEARNERS USING MULTIMEDIA?

The teacher's dilemma will not go away but some teachers seemed more easily to cope with it than others. For example, some teachers responded to the use of multimedia by exerting a high degree of control over the students' use of the machines – by providing structured worksheets – but leaving them pretty much unsupervised when actually working with the machines. This could be the worst of both worlds; too much control over the nature of the task, too little involvement with the children when carrying out the task. In contrast other teachers seemed to adopt more of a facilitator role – a hands-off approach which has gained a bad currency in some circles (e.g. Phillips 1996) as it may imply that teachers are doing very little. So what does a facilitator role look like? To be able to facilitate learning using multimedia seems to us to involve carrying out several complex and time-consuming tasks including:

- assessing proposed multimedia software for relevance and content
- gaining a level of confidence and competence in using the material for oneself
- organising access to the technology in an equitable way
- organising access to other relevant material – perhaps to other software or to library books – to support children's learning
- providing a structure or a framework towards which the group will work – in many cases this will be an open-ended task but one discussed with the group
- assessing the way that the group is negotiating its learning objectives and helping it to discuss and refine them
- assessing pupils' ability to teach others about the workings of the machine and making the need to hand over skills explicit to the pupil expert
- assessing the work of the group and suggesting appropriate activities that may lead to progression in students' learning
- reflecting on the activities of the class as a whole and acting on suggestions for amendments next time round.

Central to the facilitator role is the dialogue that goes on between teacher and the students working on the computer. This does not mean standing over the children at all times – such a task would be impossible – but it does mean engaging with learners at key moments and guiding their learning. Clearly some students working together will learn without teacher involvement (and one line of inquiry might be to examine more thoroughly what children learn through serendipitous browsing of multimedia material at home). However, creating the kinds of engagement with multimedia we have described earlier requires not only appropriate software but also the involvement of the teacher. The very least we can say of unsupervised use in schools is that it leaves learning to chance. How do we know that talk is going beyond the technical? How do we know that students are listening to each other? How do we know that new and more complex lines of inquiry are being considered? How do we know that someone is not dominating the keyboard? Instead, throughout this book we have seen the importance of teacher involvement with using multimedia in developing reading skills (Chapter 3), within information handling (Chapter 4) and in encouraging children to talk about images (Chapter 5).

The facilitator role we describe will lead teachers to be more flexible in interpreting their programmes of work. Some of the best uses of multimedia occur when learners go beyond the task which is set. We discussed how students went beyond a reading comprehension task and explored further information associated with the Vikings (pp.24–5). A problem here was that the students could see no point in doing anything with the information as it fell outside of the very narrow aims of the activity. By contrast we would like to see such work acknowledged and commented favourably upon by teachers. For example, in one school Year 7 pupils had learnt many new French vocabulary items, through using multimedia discs, which had not been predicted when the curriculum was planned. But teachers reacted favourably to this and were able to find contexts in which students could use their new vocabulary. In another example, the search for new contexts leads children to work across subject areas. A teacher had been using *Living Books* in order to develop reading skills but once she became aware of the children's enthusiasm for the software she encouraged them to produce a classroom assembly performing scenes from the living book and developed various writing and drawing activities based on the story they had seen.

AND THE FUTURE . . .

Take a centrally controlled curriculum with high subject boundaries. Add a small number of multimedia systems. Provide a sprinkling of multimedia discs which take time to get to know and longer to integrate into your teaching. Place in classrooms in which routines and practices are often strongly established. Stir a little, and wait . . . and wait.

The picture which emerges from the third part of this book is that we have not got a recipe for an educational revolution. So do we expect anything to change? The answer is surprisingly a cautiously optimistic 'yes'. In part this is because we have seen (and we hope have described) the potential for multimedia to support an accessible engaging curriculum – one that appeals to young people's strengths and encourages them to take responsibility for their learning. We have also seen plenty of teacher enthusiasm for multi-media which we expect to continue. (Even if IT has not radically changed educational practices, once established, computers are rarely phased out – perhaps we should be looking for a slowly evolving curriculum change?) But the more important reason why multimedia will not go away is that, in a very rough and ready manner, schools tend to reflect the age we live in.

We saw in Chapter 6 that the use of IT in schools is driven by the children themselves. This happens in several ways. Teachers and parents may buy multimedia systems for their own children and they can see the oppor-tunities that CD-ROM offers. They may learn how to use machines from their own children and can trial and discuss software with them. We have also seen that children bring rising expectations to school; they want to use multimedia and they help implement multimedia into the curriculum by taking on the task of training each other in its use. Their enthusiasm sustains the teacher's interest in developing further activities around IT. But changes do not just filter through into schools, sometimes the process is more explicit.

The educational journalist Peter Wilby (1996) in a review of teaching methods concluded that 'What really counted was that hard work, firm direc-tion, competition and lots of testing fitted the spirit of the 1980s and 1990s as surely as the progressive ideas fitted the 1960s.' Of course this is, as Wilby acknowledges, a caricature – where, for example, outside of some schools in the primary sector were the self-consciously libertarian schools of the 1960s? The point, though, is a good one, schools do move with the spirit of the times. The question is 'What times do we live in and what type of schools will equip us for these times?'

We are living in an age in which visual literacy is as important as print literacy, an age characterised by ever-increasing globalisation, access to growing amounts of information, continuous change and hence uncertainty as to our place in society. (This is a snapshot of a wider picture which has been discussed by many commentators, including, in the context of post-modernity and education: Hargreaves 1994.) A particular feature of these new times is the rise of the learning society and the learning organisation. Central to both concepts is the idea that the economic institutions which flourish are ones which are collaborative, flexible, global and relish the chal-lenge of innovating in situations where there can be little certainty. In such enterprises it is argued knowledge (knowledge of where to access informa-tion, how to process it and how to act on it) becomes the greatest asset. (For a further discussion over the changes required within educational institutions to match these new economic conditions, see National Commission on Education 1993.)

We recognise that there is a lively debate over the way we describe our society and that the relationship between school, society and economic organisation is a complex one. However, if we want to think of the skills that learners need to acquire – in particular, to use Kenneth Baker's pitch, the skills to provide young people with jobs – we need a curriculum supported by multimedia and other new technologies such as electronic communications software.

These skills are not simply associated with learning how to operate a computer but, more importantly, include the ability to collaborate with colleagues, to access and select from large stores of information, to have insight into the ways in which new knowledge is acquired, to take responsibility for one's own learning, to understand how image can clarify and distort. These are precisely the skills that we believe are promoted by the type of guided exploration with multimedia for which we have argued. The challenge we face is to develop a new curriculum for new times.

Appendices

Appendix 1

Glossary

analogue signal that does not vary in discrete steps, but passes continuously from one level to another. For storage, processing and communicating with computers, analogue signals are converted into digital form using analogue to digital converters (ADC). This is called digitisation, as the information is then stored in binary code.

bit a '0' or '1', used for binary code (from *bi*nary digi*t*).

byte eight bits making up a piece of binary code, e.g. 11010111, used to store or send information digitally.

CD compact disc: optical disc developed for the storage of digital audio. It has evolved into many variants such as CD-ROM, CD-I, etc.

CD-I compact disc-interactive: multimedia system developed by Philips.

CD-ROM compact disc-read only memory: typically a 12 cm diameter optical disc with data capacity of hundreds of Mbytes, e.g. 550 Mb, equivalent to about 250,000 pages of text. First announced in 1983.

CD-ROM drive device for reading CD-ROM discs: it can be portable, stand-alone or integral to a computer/multimedia system. All high specification variants read audio CDs.

CD-ROM XA compact disc-read only memory extended architecture: published by Microsoft, Philips and Sony in March 1988, permits 'near' CD-I title to be delivered using a conventional desktop computer with installed CD-ROM drive and CD-ROM XA decoder.

CDTV Commodore Dynamic Total Vision: consumer multimedia system based on Amiga connected to CD-ROM drive. World's first consumer multimedia system launched in 1991.

CMC   computer-mediated communication: using computers and communication networks to compose, process, store and deliver information that can benefit 'networked learners'.

compression   method by which computer data of any kind (often image data) are scaled down, consuming less storage space and providing a means for increased data transfer rate.

digital   signal in precise, discrete steps that can be coded using bits (0s and 1s) into binary code.

DVI   digital video interactive: video compression and decompression technology.

e-mail   electronic mail: transmission and reception of material via electronic networks. Often, a computer fitted with a modem (*mo*dulator *dem*odulator) is used for transmission and reception via telephone lines.

electronic storyboard   computer equivalent of a 'storyboard', used for developing multimedia material. It can give an overview of 'paths' through the material, possibilities for user interaction and so on.

gigabyte   1,000 million or 10^9 bytes.

GUI   graphical user interface – 'gooey': a user interface consisting of icons, allowing interaction via a mouse and minimal keyboard use. Sometimes referred to as 'front-end' or just 'user interface'.

hard disc   magnetic mass storage device consisting of a fixed disc inside a computer system (removable versions are available but most are fixed). Storage capacities are increasing continuously, currently measured in gigabytes.

hyper-link   link words or 'hot words' in hypertext which lead the reader on to other related information.

hypermedia   broader version of the hypertext concept where text is combined with images. The terms hypermedia and multimedia are sometimes seen as interchangeable.

hypertext   now widely used term, coined in the 1960s by Ted Nelson to describe the idea of linking textual information and presenting it in a non-linear fashion. Users can 'navigate' their way through it and follow their own path.

icon   symbolic, pictorial representation of any function or task.

ISDN   integrated services digital network: an international digital telecommunications standard developed to enable transmission of simultaneous high-bandwidth data, video and voice signals (all digital).

IV   interactive video: joining of video and computer technology. A video programme and a computer program run in tandem under the control of the user. In interactive video, the user's actions, choices and decisions genuinely affect the way in which the programme unfolds (see Nebraska Scale of Interaction).

IVIS   Interactive Video in Schools project.

kilobyte   1,024 or 2^{10} bytes. Often taken to mean 1,000 bytes (wrongly, strictly speaking).

Laservision   standard videodisc player and disc format developed by Philips. Manufactured by Philips and other manufacturers (e.g. Pioneer), commonly used in interactive video (IV).

medium, media and multimedia   The shorter *OED* entry under 'medium' gives a variety of definitions including a middle course, an average, and a mediator for departed spirits. It also gives the historical scientific definition of 'an intervening substance through which a force acts or impressions are conveyed to the senses'. This relates to the old belief in science that all waves, including light, require a medium (the 'ether') in which to travel. Perhaps the most useful definition in this context is of a medium as 'an intermediate agency, means, instrument or channel' – a kind of a go-between. In this sense we could see a meaning for the word 'medium' in education as a means of connecting a learner to teaching or learning material (a go-between).

However, the situation is complicated by the common usage of media as a synonym for medium – despite the fact that the former is the plural form of the latter! We often talk of 'the media', simply to mean newspapers, television, radio and so on. Further confusion arises when the term 'media' is used in education sometimes to describe:

- the technology itself in a learning situation, e.g. the TV, the VCR, the audio recorder, the personal computer
- the 'platform' for storing or 'delivering' the learning material, e.g. the tape, disc, paper, photograph, slide (as in the 1970s notion of a 'multimedia package')
- the form of the message, e.g. audio, visual, graphical, textual, pictorial.

These are all usages to watch for; it is pointless being pedantic or attempting to provide a watertight definition. To paraphrase two points from Wittgenstein's view of language (in *Philosophical Investigations*) the meaning of a word is its usage; although we may not be able to define an 'elephant' we all know one when we see one.

megabyte (Mb)   strictly speaking 1,024 kilobytes (approximately 1 million or 10^6 bytes).

MHz   mega Hertz: 1 million cycles or pulses per second. Often used to describe the clock speed of computers, providing an indication of speed of operation, e.g. a 33 MHz machine will run at 33 million clock cycles per second.

Nebraska Scale of Interaction   varying degrees (usually up to three levels) of interactivity which are, or might be, available with IV or other multimedia systems (proposed by the Nebraska Videodisc Design Group in 1980).

- Level 1:   allows stop/start; forward and reverse; freeze frame and slow motion – but limited memory and processing power
- Level 2:   as in Level 1 but with some branching, and a little computer control
- Level 3:   computer control of video, according to student needs and responses
- Level 4:   instant replies to any questions, e.g. through networks to other computers (NB: this level has *not* been agreed as a standard).

optical videodisc   videodisc that uses a laser light beam to read information from the surface of the disc. The information in optical videodiscs is encoded in the form of microscopic pits pressed into the disc surface. The pits or holes affect the laser beam in a manner that can be decoded by the videodisc player. Information stored in these pits is 'read' by laser beam and transmitted to a decoder in the player.

Photo CD   system developed by Eastman Kodak for adding up to 100 35 mm images onto a CD-ROM which can be accessed by a computer's CD-ROM drive, a CD-I player or a specially modified CD audio player.

RAM   random access memory: the part of a computer's memory that can both read (find and display) and write (record) information, and can be updated or amended by the user.

ROM   read-only memory: computer storage medium that allows the user to recall and use information (read) but *not* record or amend it (write).

surrogate travel   a multimedia application in which physical travel is simulated, allowing the user to control the path taken through the environment (e.g. a surrogate walk).

videodisc   generic term describing a medium of information storage that uses thin circular discs of varying formats, on which video, audio and data signals may be encoded (usually along a spiral track) for playback on a video monitor.

virtual reality computer-generated 'reality' that users may 'enter' using devices such as 'data gloves' and head-mounted computer graphic displays or by a multimedia system.

Appendix 2

Discography

Anglo-Saxons (1993) Schools Direct
Breakaway Maths (1997) Leeds: Yorkshire International Thomson Multimedia
The Chemistry Set (1995) London: New Media
Creative Writer (1994) Leeds: Yorkshire International Thomson Multimedia
Creepy Crawlies (1993) New Milton: Education Interactive Ltd
Dangerous Creatures (1994) Wokingham: Microsoft Press
Dinosaurs (1994) Wokingham: Microsoft Press
Directions 2000 (1993) Academy Television
Discovering India (1995) Action Aid
Domesday Project (1986) BBC, Acorn, Philips
Earth and Universe (1992) Bradford: Bradford Technology Ltd
Ecodisc (1992) New Milton: Education Interactive Ltd
Electricity and Magnetism (1993) Bradford: Bradford Technology Ltd
Elements (1994) Leeds: Yorkshire International Thomson Multimedia
Encarta: the complete interactive multimedia (1995) Wokingham: Microsoft
    Press
Exploring Nature (1994) Cumana Ltd
Eyewitness Encyclopaedia of Science and *Eyewitness Encyclopaedia of Nature*
    (1994) London: Dorling Kindersley
Forces and Effects (1996) Bradford: Bradford Technology Ltd
Frontier 2000 (1994) Rickitts Educational Media
Grolier Encyclopaedia (1995) New Milton: Education Interactive Ltd
The Guardian (1995) Chadwyck-Healey Ltd
Heather Hits a Home Run (1993) New Milton: Education Interactive Ltd
History of the World (1994), London: Dorling Kindersley
Hutchinson Encyclopaedia (1992) Cumana Ltd
The Independent (1995) Chadwyck-Healey Ltd
Information Finder (1994) Wokingham: World of Education Ltd
The Interactive Periodic Table (1993) Oxford: Attica Cybernetics Ltd
Just Grandma and Me (1993) SSVC/Broderbund Living Books
Kingfisher Children's Micropedia (1994) ESM/NCET

Le Carnaval des Animaux (1992) Cambridge: Xploratorium, Anglia Polytechnic
    University
Macbeth (1995) London: HarperCollins
Materials (1994) Leeds: Yorkshire International Thomson Multimedia
Motion: A Visual Database (1989) Cambridge: Cambridge Science Media
Moving Gives Me a Stomach Ache (1993) SSVC/Broderbrund Living Books
Musical Instruments (1993) Wokingham: Microsoft Press
New Scientist (1955) East Grinstead, Sussex: IPC/Bowker-Saur
NGS Mammals (1990) London: National Geography Society
The Paper Bag Princess (1993) New Milton: Education Interactive Ltd
Planetary Taxi (1993) TAG Developments Ltd
Pris sur le vif (1993) ScottForesman
The Secret Garden (1994) Sound Source Interactive
Sherston's Naughty Stories (1994) Malmesbury, Wiltshire: Sherston Software
Siville (1986) Interactive Video in Schools
Space Encyclopaedia (1994) Cumana Ltd
Stowaway (1994) London: Dorling Kindersley
The Times and The Sunday Times (1994) News Multimedia Ltd
The Tortoise and the Hare (1993) London: Random House UK Ltd
The Ultimate Haunted House (1995) New Milton: Education Interactive Ltd
The Ultimate Human Body (1994) London: Dorling Kindersley
Volcanoes (1989) BBC Enterprises/Oxford University Press
World Atlas (1993) Rickitts Educational Media
World of Number (1993) Henley-on-Thames: New Media

CD-ROM suppliers and producers

Anglia Multimedia
Anglia House
Norwich
Norfolk NR1 3JG
☎ 01603 615 151

Attica Cybernetics Ltd
Unit 2 Kings Meadow
Ferry Hinksey Road
Oxford OX2 0DP
☎ 01865 791 346

BTL (Bradford Technology Ltd)
   Publishing
Business and Innovation Centre
Angel Way
Listerhills
Bradford BD7 1BX
☎ 01274 841 320

Cambridge Science Media
354 Mill Road
Cambridge CB1 3NN
☎ 01223 357 546
Fax: 01223 573 994

Dorling Kindersley
53–57 Chandos Place
London WC2N 4HS
☎ 0171 836 5411

Education Interactive Ltd
Old Milton Green
New Milton
Hinton
Dorset BH25 6QJ
☎ 01425 621 218

HarperCollins
77–85 Fulham Palace Road
London W6 8JB
☎ 0181 741 7070

Main Multimedia
16 City Road
Winchester SO23 8SD
☎ 01962 870 680

Maris Multimedia Ltd
99 Mansell Street
London E1 8AX
☎ 0171 488 1566

Microsoft Press
Winnersh Triangle
Wokingham
Berks RG11 5TP
☎ 0118 927 0001
☎ 0345 002 000

New Media Press Ltd
PO Box 4441
Henley-on-Thames
Oxon RG9 3YR
☎ 01491 414 243

Projection Visual Communications
33–41 Dallington Street
London EC1V 0BB
☎ 0171 250 1706

Random House UK Ltd
20 Vauxhall Bridge Road
London SW1V 2SA
☎ 0171 973 9000

World of Education Ltd
Market House
19–21 Market Place
Wokingham
Berks RG40 1AP
☎ 0118 977 3423

Yorkshire International
Thomson Multimedia
(YITM) Ltd/ILP
The Television Centre
Leeds LS3 1JS
☎ 0113 243 8283

References

Ambron, S. and Hooper, K. (eds) (1990) *Learning with Interactive Multimedia*, Washington, DC: Microsoft Press.

Atkins, M. (1993) Theories of learning and multimedia applications: an overview, *Research Papers in Education* 8(2): 251–71.

Atkins, M. and Blissett, G. (1990) Learning activities and interactive videodisc: an exploratory study, *British Journal of Educational Technology* 20(1): 47–56.

Ayton, J. (1996) Ways of seeing and reading, *2020* 4: 21–3.

Barker, J. and Tucker, R. (eds) (1990) *The Interactive Learning Revolution: Multimedia in Education and Training*, London: Kogan Page.

Barnes, D. (1979) *From Communication to Curriculum*, Harmondsworth: Penguin.

Bennett, J. (1979) *Learning to Read with Picture Books*, Stroud: Thimble Press.

Berger, J. (1972) *Ways of Seeing*, Harmondsworth: Penguin.

BESA (1995) *UK Schools Survey on Budget and Resource Provision*, London: British Educational Suppliers Association.

Blease, D. (1986) *Evaluating Educational Software*, London: Croom Helm.

Bliss, J., Chandra, P. and Cox, M. (1986) The introduction of computers into a school, *Computers and Education* 10: 49–54.

Botto, F. (1992) *Multimedia, CD-ROM and Compact Disc: A Guide for Users and Developers*, Wilmslow: Sigma Press.

Bratt, P. and McCormick, S. (1987) *The Ecodisc: User Guide*, London: BBC.

Buckingham, D. (1993) *Children Talking Television: The Making of Television Literacy*, London: Falmer Press.

Bullock, Sir A. (1975) *A Language for Life: Report of the Committee of Inquiry into Reading and the Use of English*, London: HMSO.

Burns, C. (1995) Talking IT up, *Educational Computing and Technology* February.

Chambers, A. (1983) *Introducing Books to Children*, London: Heinemann Educational.

Chandler, D. (1983) *Young Learners and the Microcomputer*, Milton Keynes: Open University.

Clegg, C. (1994) Psychology and information technology: the study of cognition in organisations, *British Journal of Psychology* 85: 449–77.

Collins, J. (1996) *The Quiet Child*, London: Cassell.

Cook, G. (1992) *The Discourse of Advertising*, London: Routledge.

Coren, G. (1994) Access a story, Daddy, *The Times* Weekend 31 December.

Cuban, L. (1986) *Teachers and Machines: The Classroom Use of Technology since 1920*, New York: Teachers College Press.

DfE (1995) *National Curriculum Orders for English*, London: HMSO.

DfEE (1996) *Survey of IT in Schools – Statistical Bulletin*, London: DfEE.

Dyer, G. (1982) *Advertising as Communication*, London and New York: Methuen.

Ellam, N. and Wellington, J. (1986) *Computers in the Primary Curriculum*, Sheffield: USDE papers.

Fox, D. (1983) Personal theories of teaching, *Studies in Higher Education* 8(2): 151–63.

Fremantle, S. (1993) The power of the picture book, in P. Pinsent (ed.) *The Power of the Page*, London: David Fulton.

Gardner, J., Morrison, H., Jarman, R., Reilly, C. and McNally, H. (1992) *Pupils' Learning and Access to Information Technology*, School of Education, Queen's University of Belfast.

Goodman, S. (1996) Visual English, in S. Goodman and D. Graddol (eds) *Redesigning English: New Texts, New Identities*, London: Routledge.

Graham, J. (1990) *Pictures on the Page*, Sheffield: NATE.

Hammond, K., Pluim, D. and Eynde, K.V. (1995) *Interactive Mass Media: A Review of Expert Opinion and Evidence from the USA and UK*, London: Centre for Marketing, London Business School.

Hammond, M. (1994) Measuring the impact of IT on learning, *Journal of Computer Assisted Learning* 10: 251–60.

Hammond, M. (1995a) Learning from experience: approaching the research of CD-ROM in schools, in J. Tinsley and T. Van Weert (eds) *World Conference on Computers in Education VI*, London: Chapman & Hall.

Hammond, M. (1995b) Exploring a world of number, *Journal of Information Technology for Teacher Education* 4(3): 363–76.

Hannon, P. and Wooler, S. (1985) Psychology and educational computing, in J. Wellington (ed.) *Children, Computers and the Curriculum*, London: Harper & Row.

Hargreaves, A. (1994) *Changing Teachers, Changing Times*, London: Cassell.

Henderson, L. (1993) Interactive multimedia and culturally appropriate ways of learning, in C. Latchem, J. Williamson and L. Henderson-Lancett (eds) *Interactive Multimedia: Practice and Promise*, London: Kogan Page.

Heppell, S. (1993) Eyes on the horizon, feet on the ground?, in C. Latchem, J. Williamson and L. Henderson-Lancett (eds) *Interactive Multimedia: Practice and Promise*, London: Kogan Page.

Hicks, D. (1980) *Images of the World*, Occasional Paper no. 2, University of London Institute of Education.

Hofmeister, J. (1990) The birth of the hyper school, in S. Ambron and K. Hooper (eds) *Learning with Interactive Media*, Washington, DC: Microsoft Press.

Johnson, D., Cox, M. and Watson, D. (1994) Evaluating the impact of IT on pupils' achievements, *Journal of Computer Assisted Learning* 10(3): 263–6.

Keeling, R. and Whiteman, S. (1989) *Education 2010*, Birmingham: Newman Software.

Kelly, A. (1984) *Microcomputers and the Curriculum*, London: Harper & Row.

Kemmis, S. with Atkin, R. and Wright, E. (1977) *How do Students Learn?*, working papers on computer assisted learning, Norwich: Centre for Applied Research in Education, University of East Anglia.

Kress, G. and van Leeuwen, T. (1996) *Reading Images: A Grammar of Visual Communication*, London: Routledge.

Latchem, C., Williamson, J. and Henderson-Lancett, L. (eds) (1993) *Interactive Multimedia: Practice and Promise*, London: Kogan Page.

McDowell, L. (1994) The transformation of cultural geography, in D. Gregory, R. Martin and G. Smith (eds) *Human Geography: Society, Space and Social Science*, London: Macmillan.

Macfarlane, A. (1997) *IT in the Primary School*, London: Routledge.

McKeown, S. (1995) The special magic of multimedia, *Times Educational Supplement* 20 October: 16.

Mackey, M. (1996) Strip mines in the garden: old stories, new formats, and the challenge of change, *Children's Literature in Education* 27(1): 3–22.

McLaren, P. (1995) *Critical Pedagogy and Predatory Culture: Oppositional Politics in a Postmodern Era*, London: Routledge.

McLuhan, M. (1964) *Understanding Media*, London: Routledge & Kegan Paul.

Medwell, J. (1994) *Teachers' Notes for Oxford Reading Tree Softwares, Stage 2 Talking Stories*, Oxford: Sherston.

Medwell, J. (1995) Talking books for teaching reading, *Micro-Scope* autumn: 23–5.

Medwell, J. (1996) Talking books and reading, *Reading* April: 41–6.

Meek, M. (1982) *Learning to Read*, London: Bodley Head.

Megarry, J. (1990) Editorial, *British Journal of Educational Technology* 21(2): 84–94.

Mercer, N. (1995) *The Guided Construction of Knowledge: Talk amongst Teachers and Learners*, Clevedon (Avon): Multilingual Matters.

Millard, E. (1994) *Developing Readers in the Middle Years*, Milton Keynes: Open University Press.

Morgan, J. and Welton, P. (1986) *See What I Mean: An Introduction to Visual Communication*, 2nd edn, London: Edward Arnold.

National Commission on Education (1993) *Learning to Succeed: A Radical Look at Education Today and a Strategy for the Future*, London: Heinemann.

National Council for Educational Technology (NCET) (1992) *CD-ROM in Schools Scheme: Evaluation Report*, by J. Steadman, C. Nash and M. Eraut, Coventry: NCET.

NCET (1994a) *CD-ROM in Education: CD-ROM Titles Review*, Coventry: NCET.

NCET (1994b) *Integrated Learning Systems: A Report of the Pilot Evaluation of ILS in the UK*, Coventry: NCET.

NCET (1994c) *IT Works*, Coventry: NCET.

NCET (1994d) *Teaching and Learning with Interactive Media*, Coventry: NCET.

NCET (1994e) *CD-ROM in Education: The Initial Teacher Education Scheme*, Coventry: NCET.

NCET (1995) *CD-ROMs in Primary Schools: An Independent Evaluation*, Coventry: NCET.

NCET (1996) *CD-ROMs in Primary Schools: An Independent Evaluation*, by J. Collins, K. Littleton, J. Longman, N. Mercer, P. Scrimshaw and R. Wegeriff, Coventry: NCET.

Norris, N., Davies, R. and Beattie, C. (1990) Evaluating new technology: the case of the Interactive Video in Schools (IVIS) programme, *British Journal of Educational Technology* 21(2): 84–94.

Olson, J. (1988) *Schoolworlds/Microworlds: Computers and the Culture of the Classroom*, Oxford: Pergamon.

Oppenheim, C. (ed.) (1998) *CD-ROM: Fundamentals to Applications*, London: Butterworth.

Papert, S. (1993) *The Children's Machine: Rethinking School in the Age of the Computer*, New York: Basic Books.

Perzylo, L. (1993) The application of multimedia CD-ROMs in schools, *British Journal of Educational Technology* 24(3): 191–7.

Peters, R. S. (1966) *Ethics and Education*, London: George Allen & Unwin.

Phillips, M. (1996) *All Must Have Prizes*, London: Little, Brown.

Plowman, L. (1996) Narrative, linearity and interactivity: making sense of interactive multimedia, *British Journal of Educational Technology* 27(2): 92–105.

Romiszowski, A.J. (1988) *The Selection and Use of Instructional Media*, London: Kogan Page.

Rouse, C. (1994) Frontier 2000, in *Micro-Scope, Multimedia Special*, Birmingham: Newman College.

Rushby, N. (1979) *An Introduction to Educational Computing*, London: Croom Helm.

Scaife, J. and Wellington, J.J. (1993) *IT in Science and Technology Education*, Milton Keynes: Open University Press.

Schostak, J. (1988) *Breaking into the Curriculum: The Impact of IT on Schooling*, London: Methuen.

Sendov, B. (1986) The second wave: problems of computer education, in R. Ennals, R. Gwyn and L. Zdravchev (eds) *Information Technology and Education*, Chichester: Ellis Horwood.

Sewell, D. (1990) *New Tools for New Minds: A Cognitive Perspective on the Use of Computers with Young Children*, Hemel Hempstead: Harvester Wheatsheaf.

Smith, F. (1978) *Reading*, Cambridge: Cambridge University Press.

Smith, F. (1988) How education backed the wrong horse, in *Joining the Literacy Club: Further Essays into Education*, Portsmouth, NH: Heinemann.

Spender, D. (1995) *Nattering on the Net: Women, Power and Cyberspace*, Melbourne: Spinifex.

Squires, D. and McDougall, A. (1994) *Choosing and Using Educational Software*, London: Falmer Press.

Steele, R. and Wellington, J. (1985) Hardware and humans, *Times Educational Supplement* 9 March.

Taylor, P.H., Reid, W.A., Holley, B.J. and Exon, G. (1974) *Purpose, Power and Constraint in the Primary Curriculum*, London: Macmillan for the Schools Council.

Tyack, D. and Cuban, L. (1995) *Tinkering toward Utopia: A Century of Public School Reform*, Cambridge, MA: Harvard University Press.

Underwood, J. (1994) Databases, in J.D.M. Underwood (ed.) *Computer Based Learning: Potential into Practice*, London: David Fulton.

Underwood, J. and Underwood, G. (1990) *Computers and Learning*, Oxford: Basil Blackwell.

Usher, R. and Edwards, R. (1994) *Postmodernism and Education*, London: Routledge.

Walker, D.F. and Hess, R.D. (1984) *Instructional Software: Principles and Perspectives for Design and Use*, Belmont, CA: Wadsworth.

Waterland, L. (1985) *Read with Me*, Stroud: Thimble Press.

Waterland, L. (1992) The multi-layered picture book, in P. Pinsent (ed.) *The Power of the Page*, London: David Fulton.

Wellington, J. (1985) *Children, Computers and the Curriculum*, London: Harper & Row.

Wellington, J. (1989) *Education for Employment: The Place of IT*, Windsor: NFER-Nelson.

Wellington, J. (1990) The impact of IT on the school curriculum: downwards, sideways, backwards and forwards, *Journal of Curriculum Studies* 22(1): 57–63.

Wellington, J. (1991) Newspaper science, school science: friends or enemies?, *International Journal of Science Education* 13(4): 363–72.

Wellington, J. (1995) The role of new technology in teacher education: a case study of hypertext in a PGCE course, *Journal of Education for Teaching* 21(1): 37–50.

Wilby, P. (1996) Do we really want to go back to all this?, *The Independent* 1 June.

Wilson, M. (1994) The Horizon Project, in *Micro-Scope, Multimedia Special*, Birmingham: Newman College.

Winter, C. (1997) Ethnocentric bias in geography textbooks: a framework for reconstruction, in D. Tilbury and M. Williams (eds) *Teaching and Learning Geography*, London: Routledge.

Wood, D. (1988) *How Children Think and Learn: The Social Contexts of Cognitive Development*, Oxford: Basil Blackwell.

Index